PRAISE F(

In the Land of Long ⌐ ⌐⌐⌐⌐⌐⌐⌐

"Reads like a novel . . . This book feels right; that is,
it convinces us unequivocally that this is what working in
a cemetery at the end of the swinging sixties must have
been like . . . Just sit back and enjoy the show." —*Booklist*

"Wilkins distills his bizarre day-to-day into a cohesive
narrative and a compelling commentary on the times, a perfect
trip for those who weren't able to take time off work for
the Summer of Love." —*Publishers Weekly*

"If Raymond Chandler had written a memoir, I could imagine
it reading like this . . . Wilkins has worked his factual shockers
into a personal narrative as rolling and carefully landscaped
as the grounds he tended . . ." —MARY ROACH, author of *Stiff*

"Most of his adventure is purely hilarious . . . but
despite his considerable art as a humorist, Wilkins's comedy
can't help but be serious . . . The result is a note-perfect tune
to whistle past the ridiculous graveyard." —*Globe and Mail*

"A gem . . . It's the humanity at the core of the
book—plus Wilkins' gymnastic prose and laughs
aplenty—that really powers this book." —*Toronto Star*

"Rollicking, irreverent . . . riveting and squirm-
inducing all at once." —*Winnipeg Free Press*

"Seen through Wilkins's sharp, playful gaze, the business of
working with stiffs is anything but." —*Fast Forward* (Calgary)

"An enthralling memoir of a bizarre summer spent digging graves at a cemetery in Toronto." —*Ottawa Citizen*

"Wilkins provides a singularly poignant comic look behind the scenes of this gloomy business...Remarkable reading."
—*Chicago Sun-Times*

"A fascinating account... Wilkins explores the grim details of working in a cemetery and how the experience ultimately shaped his journey to adulthood." —*Library Journal*

"Wilkins is a master storyteller, and canny with a punch line..." —*Literary Review of Canada*

"Wry and stuffed with zingers." —*Toro*

"Wilkins challenges us to think about the big questions... In pretending to talk about himself, he has shown us—through corpses, graveyard gibes and all—a mirror that reflects us and our death- and life-defying culture." —*Prairie Fire*

"Readers will never look at cemeteries the same way again after this utterly fascinating and unforgettable memoir."
—*Scene Magazine* (London, ON)

"Wonderfully written... It didn't inspire Wilkins to become a mortician but it did sharpen his eye, leading to some pretty nifty observations, fluid descriptive writing and a sense of dark humour that is doubly delicious." —*The Sun Times* (Owen Sound, ON)

"I laughed until my face hurt... Life is a grotesque comedy after all, and death is, in many ways, the ultimate punch line."
—Richard Gavin, *At Fear's Altar*

IN THE LAND OF
LONG FINGERNAILS

charles wilkins

IN THE LAND
OF LONG
fingernails

A GRAVEDIGGER'S
MEMOIR

GREYSTONE BOOKS
D&M PUBLISHERS INC.
Vancouver/Toronto/Berkeley

Greystone Books
An imprint of D&M Publishers Inc.
2323 Quebec Street, Suite 201
Vancouver BC Canada V5T 4S7
www.greystonebooks.com

Cataloguing data available from Library and Archives Canada
ISBN 978-1-55365-843-6 (pbk.)
ISBN 978-1-55365-875-7 (ebook)

Cover design by Jessica Sullivan
Text design by Naomi MacDougall
Cover photograph by Alan Thornton/Stone/Getty Images
Printed and bound in Canada by Friesens
Text printed on acid-free, 100% post-consumer paper
Distributed in the U.S. by Publishers Group West

We gratefully acknowledge the financial support of the Canada Council
for the Arts, the British Columbia Arts Council, the Province of
British Columbia through the Book Publishing Tax Credit and the Government
of Canada through the Canada Book Fund for our publishing activities.

For my son, Matt, with love

AUTHOR'S NOTE

FOR FIVE months during the summer of 1969, I worked as a gravedigger and roustabout in a huge corporate cemetery in the suburbs of Toronto. The place was owned by conniving, often ruthless opportunists and was worked by the drug-addled misfits and dreamers who, for a season under the sun, were my confederates and confidants.

For reasons of discretion that I suspect will become clear, I have changed the names of every one of those people, and as much as possible have disguised my setting. I have renamed the cemetery Willowlawn Everlasting Inc. To call it by its real name in this era of inquisitional conformity would be an open invitation to, at best, a lawsuit, at worst a contract hit—on me.

Hardly a day passed between May and September of that year when I did not witness some grim new violation of civility or law, or discover some unexplored threshold in my awareness of human behaviour. But while part of me loathed the cemetery, another part revelled in its every bizarre nuance and hypocrisy: from the motto on the paycheques, "Eternal Peace, Eternal Maintenance," to the fact that the messages affixed to the tops of the concrete outer vaults—"One with the Lord," "Redeemed by

Grace" and such—were configured by the likes of myself out of size-XXL industrial Catelli Alphaghetti, or "necronoodles," as we sometimes called them.

I was fascinated, equally, by the language of the place, a functional poetry of "slay carpenters," "dirt nappers" and "cracker boxes," of "crank decks" and "sod-tops," of "sinkers" and "stinkers." And by the stories, hundreds of them—told by undertakers, gravediggers, plot salesmen: the stillborn calf in the coffin, the corpse with the shrunken head, the muttering voice beneath the sod.

Taken together, the anthropologists tell us, such tales are a repository of a subculture's values and obsessions—in this case, of those who work with the dead: their uncertainty and superstitions, their relentless gallows humour amid the inevitable reminders (more easily overlooked in the world beyond the fence) of what it is, finally, to be human.

What follows is their story, our story—the story of how proximity and circumstance redefined us during the course of our months together; of how life's pettiness, politicking and occasional grace, its wild and exotic variation, played out against the backdrop of the inevitable.

PART One

one

AND SO IT BEGINS

MONDAY MORNING at the cemetery, hangover and confusion: Peter the Dutch gravedigger high atop his massive hydraulic thunder-lizard, revving it to the deepest recesses of its innards, forcing out such putrid clouds of exhaust that nobody in the repair shop can get a lungful of breathable air; Hogjaw, Peter's Belgian assistant, ramming the tail end of a pineapple and peanut butter sandwich into his mouth, galloping across the lawn as Peter screams at him in Dutch to move his skinny *ʒitvlak* because a funeral's arriving in an hour and they haven't even marked out the grave; Scotty, the autocratic old foreman, a snappish slug-eyed little general, tossing back a three-ounce bracer of whisky to fortify himself against the day, emerging from his second-storey office and descending the stairs just in time to see his teenaged grandson mistakenly pouring latrine disinfectant into the gas tank of a brand new Lawn-Boy; Scotty firing his grandson on the spot then lurching out after him into the Garden of the Immaculate Conception, rehiring the boy if for no other reason than it will enable him to fire him the next Monday and the next; Scotty shambling back into the shop now, where Luccio, the big Calabrese doctoral candidate, is absorbing a last-minute passage of James Joyce, while over in the corner, the cemetery's one-armed gardener mixes up a batch of diabolically smelly Robusto-brand nitrates and horseshit...

It is at this point that I make my own rather impertinent appearance, a curly-headed kid with a summer job, clattering down the cemetery's main road in my decrepit Sunbeam Alpine, late as usual, fishtailing on the gravel where the pavement branches into the Garden of the Apostles of the Living Christ, coasting the last hundred feet to a halt under a spready silver maple, just as Scotty descends the stairs from his second life-sustaining gurgle of cut-rate 40-proof blended screaming *Where the hell were you?* and reminding me that the next time I'm late I'm fired once and for all, docking me a half hour's pay and ordering me to get out there pronto to help Luccio get a grave ready because the mourners are gonna be there in a gawdam wink and because the dead man is the former reeve of East Township, and so on, and so on...

Meanwhile, under the customary Monday morning cloud of laziness, pettiness, halitosis, chaos, inertia, three or four other lowly employees trudge off with the enthusiasm of ripening stiffs to begin their temporary spiritless bottom-feeding bone-head jobs, their only consolation being that, even in 90 degrees of heat, work in the cemetery is relatively easy and that if they're resourceful they can sleep two or three hours a day under the honeysuckles out by the paupers' graves where Scotty only goes when he's caught short and can't make it back to the shop to piss out all the whisky he's consumed since the day began with its customary fits, farts and befuddlements at eight o'clock in the morning.

I PROMPTLY join Luccio who is away out in the Garden of the Apostles lying reading under an ornamental willow while Peter finishes the digging. The digger is a formidable long-necked mantis of a thing with a snake's knot of intestines and a barrel-sized scoop whose teeth take a bite exactly the width of a standard grave. The machine is so strong it can crash its way through two feet of ground frost in winter. Yet Peter handles it with such delicacy that Scotty, in a rare moment of appreciation, declared one day that Peter could "change gawdam diapers with it." All very neat, except that this time Peter is rattled because the side walls of the grave keep caving in. As usual at Willow-lawn, the neighbouring graves have been dug too close in order to save space; and, sure enough, as I peer into the hole I can see the old rough boxes, single on one side, two deep on the other, the three of them as rotten as compost, the top one in danger of collapsing into the new pit.

Luccio rises on his elbow and declares that Joyce is a long-winded bore. "Fortunately the man is brilliant," he adds, "which prevents him from being an ordinary bore like you, Wilkins." He looks at me solemnly, reaches into his pocket and withdraws the tiny bag of marijuana that he carries constantly. He has a patch of the stuff growing somewhere on the back acres of the cemetery—his "secret garden" he calls it. He rolls a stout little reefer and hands it to me to light. Peter gets a whiff and comes over, then Hogjaw the Belgian who has just driven up on the tractor hauling the coffin-lowering frame and the rugs of fake grass and all the other widgets and tittybits required to get the reeve into the ground with a proper portion of dignity. One of Scotty's inarguable ordinances is that seamy earthly realities never be permitted to impinge on what he refers to as "the integrity of the rites." To that end, we are diligent in disguising any stray suggestion that, say, soil is dirty, or puddles wet, or rotting flesh or embalming chemicals anything less than another olfactory grace note in a world of honeysuckle and lilacs.

Today, to quell the stink seeping from the neighbour-ing graves, which are in effect open from the sides, Scotty has ordered the application of BalsamBlast grave disinfectant and, in order to gussy up appearances, his prized German Gratzenturf rather than plain old outdoor carpeting. The *turf*, he feels bound to remind us, is a luxury he is not obliged to provide, even at what he calls "celebrity interments." He couldn't even offer such sumptuousness, he protests, had the city's only cemetery supply dealer not recently run out of regular indoor-outdoor, enabling him to acquire Aryan superiority at pre-Hitlerian prices. The true burn for Scotty, it might be noted, is that there actually *are* no celebrity interments at Willowlawn, the jockeys and mobsters and whisky magnates of the city having for decades preferred burial among the more influential stiffs in, say, Pine Hills or Mount Pleasant, *real* cemeteries, where the tonnage of marble alone makes it considerably less likely that the place will one day be excavated, its swamp of embalming chemicals purged from the soil, to make way for the "gracious duplexes" and "affordable executive estates" that are spreading across the city like a contagion.

Peter smokes earnestly and heads off on the digger to pick up the concrete outer-vault that goes into the grave before the coffin. In this Age of Aquarius, with its implied ethic of a return to the land, it is a succulent little irony for Luccio that such vaults have become a standard appurtenance among those who, even in the depths of the grave, snuggled tight to eternity, refuse a reintroduction to the soil. At the same time, the vaults have become the subject of conjecture among death industry capitalists and city planners, who are not entirely convinced that the carcasses of even the worthiest corporate monkeys should be stored in perpetuity in A-bomb–proof vaults beneath gazillion-dollar real estate that, ideally, should be easing its inhabitants back to nature and should itself eventually be returned to the common good.

Luccio takes a last long tow on the reefer—you can almost smell his fingers burning. He gets up and flicks the roach into the grave, stands reflective with his hands on his hips. He breathes deep, the Colossus of Hades. "If I'd written *Ulysses*," he snorts into the wind, "I'd've made the damn thing worth reading!" In me, he has an appreciative audience for his bull and is perpetually adding fuel to the half-assed literary debate we've had going since way back in early May. Beneath his apparent disdain for this writer or that one is a passion for literature that keeps him reading five, six hours a day. Even in the few months I've known him he has consumed a wildly erratic syllabus of fiction, eroticism, philosophy: Henry Miller, Terry Southern, Simone de Beauvoir, Carson McCullers, Mickey Spillane, Malcolm Lowry . . . the Bible, Behan, Sartre. And now of course Joyce. His formal education is in economics—and a prodigious education it is. He has a master's degree from the University of Bologna and another from Columbia in New York. At the moment he is awaiting word on his doctoral thesis from the University of Pennsylvania. He works in the graveyard for $2.10 an hour while downtown a panel of executives considers his application for a job in the investment offices of Imperial Oil. "If they've got any balls," he tells me, "they'll gimme the job, no ifs or buts." Forty thousand he expects to make, declaring that when he gets his first cheque he'll go straight out to buy a Fiat firewagon and a couple of Armani suits.

Meanwhile Scotty's little green Vauxhall comes over the rise and we all hop to it, shovelling, raking, sweeping, generally making things presentable while the reeferbuzz comes slowly to our temples and ears.

Today, because it is threatening rain and because the dead man is something of a personage, we have been ordered to raise the big green canopy over the grave—always a pain. Hogjaw unrolls it on the lawn.

Scotty approaches, all sails flapping, and immediately spies Luccio's book. "I thought I told ya t' get ridda the damn thing!" he bristles.

"Different book," sniffs Luccio.

"Same piss-poor effort!" says Scotty, and marches back to his car where he keeps a flask of Scotch in the glove compartment. *"You've got twenty minutes to get the canopy up!"* he hollers from the road.

After a flurry of phony enthusiasm, Luccio saunters over to his book, plunks himself down and resumes his reading, punctuating it with periodic snorts and guffaws. He is both a medicine and a disease, this guy—a tonic to the likes of me, a blight to everyone and everything even remotely responsible or respectable. "He's a verrry sick young man," Scotty muttered to me one day as he enumerated Luccio's countless crimes and affronts against Willowlawn, God and humanity (in all of whose images Scotty is inclined to see himself).

During my second day on the job I asked Luccio casually if anybody ever opened the coffins before the graves were filled. Immediately, he jumped into a grave, turned the coffin screws with a nickel and flipped open the box, exposing a drastically shrunken old crone with a visible mortician's stitch in her lips, and hands that had been reduced, apparently by disease, to something approximating herons' feet. "Death is beautiful," he whispered up at me. "Fuck," he said, "she's still got her pearls on. I'm surprised the rag-and-bone man hasn't been around," and he banged down the lid, producing a gun-like crack, oak on oak, the satin padding that might have prevented such sharpness having been stuffed inside for final descent into what Luccio refers to as "the peace that passeth misunderstanding."

"The rag-and-bone man," it should be pointed out, is our own brother Hogjaw, Teamster Number 6233, who because he once swiped a Rolex off the wrist of an embalmed dentist has a largely concocted reputation as a guy who would steal anything off a corpse, up to and including false teeth, spectacles, jewellery, toupees, war medals, glass eyes, monocles, gold fillings,

Masonic regalia, rosaries and Holy Bibles. The last two of these, Peter likes to say, are placed in the hands of dead believers as a sort of eleventh-hour lawn sign before the election, a stroke of late campaigning, on the off chance that the God of Endless Love might be wavering over the fate of the deceased, might be leaning toward the Long Shivaree and might be vulnerable to the subliminal messages of the contents of the coffin.

"You're a gawdam idiot," blusters Scotty on hearing this, and he proceeds to explain in his drunken Scottish burr that the placement of the rosary or Holy Bible in such a circumstance is "a merre comforrrt" to those who mourrn, although by no means as comforrrting, he would tell you, as, say, a trrriple Scotch or the thought that the last will and testament might include a little extrra crrream in its sour disperrrsal of the milk of human kaindness.

"I don't see how anybody could wear the watch off a stiff," says Scotty's grandson, David, drawing a pained look from Luccio who, having completed his reassessment of the teenager's intelligence, explains patiently that Hogjaw "didn't *wear* the watch, brainbox, he sold it!" and that the only reason he didn't steal the suits and dresses is "that they're split up the arse in such a way that the best Italian tailor in the world couldn't put them back together."

Luccio has been in the city six months and remains not because he likes it but because his sister is here and because his student visa has run out and he can no longer live in the United States. His citizenship is Italian. He is having visa problems in Canada too, though he hopes the people at Imperial will sort them out. He lives with his sister in a dinky apartment in the suburbs and takes the bus ten miles to work every day. It isn't the life he dreamed of at Columbia but is better than selling "miracle" brooms door-to-door as he did after he arrived here from Pennsylvania. He told me one day that in two weeks of selling he managed to get rid of only two brooms for a gross income of fourteen dollars—which was in fact a net loss since his peddling licence cost him ten dollars and the brooms three-fifty each. "And besides," he says, "I buggered up my running shoes. The only thing they're good for now is gravedigging."

"And reading Joyce."

"Yes, yes," he says, "and marathon self-abuse—the joys of *Gent Magazine*," and he screams out a few strains of Italian opera.

The remarkable thing about Luccio is that, whatever else is happening, he manages to remain cheerful, even clownish. The only times I see him depressed are the times when he's reminded that he hasn't been with a woman for three or four months. And even these bouts are usually brief. "Wilkins," he'll say to me, "I need a woman—what am I gonna do?"

"Go get one."

"I oughta go downtown and get myself a good hooker."

"Go," I tell him.

"Can't afford it."

"Get a girlfriend."

"Can't afford it."

This sort of thing continues for a few minutes, leading eventually into a maundering reminiscence about the prostitutes in Naples or his old girlfriends in New York and how sensational they were, etc., etc. And before long his mood has taken a turn and his cheerfulness is back, and he has more or less buried his despondency.

One weekend, in an attempt to get him serviced, I took him to a party at the university. Unfortunately, of the two girls he met, one was inseparable from her sociology professor, the other too dim to appreciate his unusual talents and personality. "If I were a broad," he said to me on the way home, "I'd fuck all the time. I'd never stop." His deprived sensibilities have been confused by some notion that women can find desirable partners any time they happen to want them. Perpetual satisfaction. And he can't even get a nibble. By way of moral support I offer up my own simple view of the mating lottery, a perspective derived of a number of minor heartbreaks and refusals, the gist of it being that some women appreciate you and some don't, and that's the way it is, and there's nothing you can do to change it.

AGAINST EVERY law of physics and trigonometry we succeed in getting the canopy up, although when I stand back to check its angles I see that it looks more like a drunken daddy longlegs than a peaceful shelter for a family of mourners. The canvas is flapping crazily, and the poles and guy ropes are straining every which way against the wind. Peter returns on the digger with the concrete outer-vault, but because of the canopy he can't get close enough to the grave to lower the thing, and we have to take everything down and start over. However, this time it's a race against the clock—as well as the storm which is fast approaching. We scurry around like contestants in some wacky television game and accomplish in seven or eight minutes what would normally take half an hour. Hogjaw throws down the artificial grass, Peter the lowering frame. Together they crank up the frame so that its straps are tight enough to take the weight of the coffin. A black station wagon arrives carrying twenty or thirty floral bouquets from the funeral home. The driver is an apprentice undertaker of about eighteen who goes about his work with long stiff-legged strides. I help him cart the bouquets over to the grave and as I put each one down he fiddles with it so the effect is just so. He's somewhat agawk that we're only now finishing with the preparations and asks if we're aware that the funeral is on its way.

"We've been waiting for it since six this morning!" barks Peter. "If it doesn't come soon we're gonna put all this shit away, and you can bury him yourself!"

The canopy stakes are two-foot lengths of rebar, and as a last measure of security, Luccio takes the sledgehammer and knocks them a little further into the ground. Peter tells him not to, but he pays no attention, and suddenly everything has been pulled so tight that there is an audible popping of threads, at first just a few, then dozens, hundreds, accelerating, so that within seconds a five-foot split has opened right down the centre seam of the canvas. It's as if the sky itself had been ripped open. The young undertaker is almost in tears. Scotty has warned us a hundred times about stretching the canopy too tight. Luckily he's unlikely to see it, as he doesn't generally go too close to the prepared graves. According to Peter he's afraid he'll fall in and we won't let him out, which in a sense does represent his point of view. Scotty is well over seventy and doesn't want any gratuitous reminders that he's soon enough going to be lowered into a muddy grey hole. He wants even less to be reminded that the lowering will be conducted by his own patchy employees. Yes, old Scotty owns a burial plot right here in Willowlawn, a family plot no less, a princely little perk of his decades of commitment to the disposal of the dead. But he keeps its location a dark secret. He's afraid, says his grandson, that one of us might "bugger it up"—and his apprehension may be justified. Peter once told me that, when the Happy Day arrived, he and Hogjaw intended to piss on Scotty's grave until the soil was so caustic and filth-ridden that not a weed or flower or blade of grass could survive on it. Of course Scotty would do the same to Peter and Hogjaw if there were any way to accomplish it short of murder, or including murder.

We immediately slacken the guy ropes, taking tension off the torn seam but inadvertently freeing up the rest of the canopy, so that the whole thing is now slapping at its own flaps and tatters.

"Maybe you should take it down," says the undertaker.

"Maybe you should put a cork in it!" says Peter.

Everybody looks at Peter for direction.

"To hell with it," he snarls. "Let's get outta here." And we quickly sweep up and throw the implements onto the wagon. Peter roars off toward the shop on the digger, Hogjaw close behind on the tractor.

Luccio and I walk casually up to the statuary garden at the top of the rise while the young undertaker fusses with the grave. Finally he has everything right—except for the rip of course and the near-constant flapflap of the canvas.

Luccio ducks behind some shrubs, lights a smoke, pulls out his book. I shake a pebble from my boot as Fred the one-armed gardener emerges from the rose bushes gesticulating skyward and yattering away in pidgin English—something about the weather. He joins us for a cigarette while the Apostles of the Living Christ glare down from the corners of the garden, their concrete eyes brimming with disapproval. The cemetery is littered with third-rate statuary: the Apostles, the Prophets, the Poets, the Patriarchs, the Virgin . . . and smack in the middle of them all an enormous sad depiction of the Lord Jesus Christ, looking as disgruntled and stupefied as the rest of us over his surroundings.

Fred gestures skyward and attempts earnestly to communicate. He knows about a hundred words of English and reminds me of some misshapen peasant out of a Brueghel painting. His work clothes are practically solid with grease and his lone arm hangs nearly to his knees. It's about as close as Scotty ever comes to a joke to say that Fred should get only half pay because of his arm ha-ha. If there were justice he'd get double pay; he does twice as much work with one arm as any of the rest of us accomplish with two. I asked him once how he lost the arm and when he didn't understand I reached out and patted his shoulder stub and gestured with my hands in puzzlement. He immediately thrust out his arm and sighted down it as if it were a rifle. "Blam!" he shouted. Peter talks a bit of German with him and tells me Fred was a resistance fighter in Poland during the war and spent three or four years in a German prison camp. In winter he works part-time, doing whatever jobs he can with one hand. In spring he gets ready for summer, and in fall he gets ready for spring. But there is only one season of any real distinction to him—summer, when the gardens are in bloom and his hand and knees are filthy with soil.

THE FUNERAL procession winds through the main part of the cemetery—a fat black snake, glittering and self-important. Scotty leads it along in his frog-green Vauxhall knowing that if he slows down even a smidgen it will nip him on the backside. He weaves just a little under the whisky.

The three of us watch from a distance, Luccio and I staying low because we're supposed to be trimming hedges during the service. It is Scotty's unaccountable claim that he never gets anything but a full workday out of his employees—every minute a work minute.

Just as the coffin is being unloaded, the wind begins to drop, so that barely a minute later everything is hush. It is the calm before the storm, and for reasons of fortuitous timing it takes on an eerie-seeming significance. The canopy hangs limp over the grave; the sky blackens dramatically. Everything is so quiet that even fifty yards away we can hear the dispassionate drone of the minister's voice, this against the sporadic grumble of thunder.

> . . . *Thou turnest men back to dust,*
> *and sayest, Turn back O children of men!* . . .

The service goes off without a hitch, and is just over when again the wind begins to churn, the lightning to crack out of the sky. A minute later the storm hits full fury. The mourners scatter for their cars, and Fred, Luccio and I run for cover under a tall blue spruce. It is the wrong thing to do on account of the lightning, but I haven't the focus or inclination to make the point. We huddle up so close that, by the time the storm eases, Luccio and I are half-petrified by the garlic on Fred's breath. We are also just as wet as if we'd avoided the tree altogether and stretched out on the lawn for fifteen minutes.

Luccio and I slog over to the grave to discover that the canopy has been ripped wide open by the wind. Luccio lets out a war whoop and hauls it to the ground. He flips the latch on the lowering frame and the walnut coffin slides into the grave, clunking as it hits the concrete. Peter arrives on the digger, Hogjaw following on the tractor with the wagon. Peter's mood has improved and he is singing loudly in Dutch. He has a shrill tenor voice. Soon Hogjaw is singing in French and Luccio in Italian. Against the growl of the digger and the clatter of wheelbarrows and implements (and in the mellowing warp of the marijuana), their combined voices sound like some elaborate new-wave requiem. "Death," Luccio pauses to inform us, "is the first and final phase of the Ultimate Democracy." He peels off his shirt and pants and tosses them onto the low branch of a birch tree to dry. He is wearing baby-blue jockey shorts, in which his underemployed shlong bulges like a length of mortadella. "In the land of the sod-topped sky," he declaims quietly, "even a lazy *Calabrazy* like me has a half-assed shot at redemption."

Luccio and I dismantle the canopy while Hogjaw removes the lowering frame and the premium indoor-outdoor. When everything is cleared back, Peter attaches a cable to the lid of the concrete vault and hoists it on the digging bucket. He tosses me a caulking gun. I tighten its pressure screw, kick the mud off my boots and lower myself into the grave. There is water on the lid of the coffin, and as I work I twice come close to flipping off my feet. Edging my way around, I spread caulking tar on the upper edge of the vault. Finished, I hoist myself out and Peter lowers the lid, which emits a small splish as it hits the tar: the reeve of East Township sealed tight against eternity.

By the time two tons of clay have been plowed in on top of him, the sun is shining and the wind has swung from east to west.

Peter and Hogjaw take off on their vehicles, and Luccio and I trudge up to the shop for our coffee break. We cut through the potter's field along the far fences—the cheapest graves in paradise—through the Garden of Gethsemane, into the Garden of the Last Supper and the most expensive graves affluence can buy.

two

THE LUXURIATING HARMONY

OF THE PEACEABLE KINGDOM

AT NOON sharp, Luccio and I leap into my old Alpine, a moulder-
ing wreck of a sports car, and clatter off to Paletta's Sport Bar
for lunch. We're no sooner through the door when Paletta tears
into Luccio in a fit of operatic Italian. Luccio lashes back, then
pulls out his wallet and, in a grand gesture, throws a handful of
bills onto the bar. He sees that one of them is bigger than he'd
intended, snatches it back and stuffs it into his pants pocket. The
two glare at one another, neither backing off, until Paletta's wife
emerges from the kitchen and returns the money to Luccio, who
by this time has ascended into a self-righteous snit and is all but
oozing rectitude.

"What'll it be?" she says quietly as she ushers us to a table by
the window.

"Double meatball on a bun," sniffs Luccio. "With provolone.
And extra sauce. And a little parmesan. And a Brio. And an
extra roll. And some butter."

The argument, it turns out, is over a dope transaction—
Luccio has supplied Paletta with an ounce from his private

harvest. "One week it's good, the next it's *inferiore*," he scoffs, laying the blame squarely on his friend's habit of cutting "every little bud with half a fucking bale of tobacco." Paletta, according to Luccio, is too cheap even to buy papers, preferring to roll his smoke in little flaxen pages torn from the Gideon New Testament that was given to him as an elementary school student. "Ecclesiastical slims," deadpans Luccio, adding that Paletta is the only man in history to have inhaled the entire Revelation of St. John the Divine.

A minute later Paletta appears at the table muttering apologetically in Italian. Luccio mutters back and gets up to make his daily call home to see if his letter from Imperial has arrived— his magical letter, the mystical epistle that will put wings on his heels, and Zegna suits and hundred-dollar pajamas on his back.

But of course it hasn't arrived.

"Foosball?" says Paletta as we finish up, and, after a momentary pause to decide whether he has entirely forgiven his countryman, Luccio rises with a snort and takes his place at the mechanical soccer game, where the two of them plunge into intense voiceless combat.

On the way back to work, the coat hanger that holds up the exhaust system on the car lets loose, setting up a din—sparks flying, everybody rubbernecking as we go balling down St. Clair toward the cemetery.

THE AFTERNOON is a marathon of grass clipping—all the stray grass around the stones, where the power mowers can't get to it. Talk has never been cheaper. Luccio eventually gets onto his Ph.D., about as suffocating a rumour as you could hope to avoid on a day in June. Like all unfinished degrees, especially the big ones, it's a kind of sickness in his gut, won't leave him alone. His dissertation is a long-winded abstraction, a formula actually, by which he hopes to describe the economic prospects of so-called underdeveloped countries. Social conditions, politics, climate, history, native bellicosity, natural resources . . . ganja, poppy seed, palm wine; they're all part of the model, which is so complicated even Luccio despairs of trying to explain it—at least to me: factors on top of functions on top of factors. I ask him if the formula works and he stands there hustling his balls, a faint smile on his face. It occurs to me that he doesn't actually care whether it works, or about economics at all. I put it to him, and he submits that economists as a rule are about a notch above skunks on the scale of vertebrate allure—"two above guys like you," he cannot resist adding.

Part of him would love to kick over the whole business, to tell his professors where to put it all and how far up. They've tyrannized him for years and for what?—the possibility of an ulcerating job and a few suits and a car.

"And women," he reminds me. "If you have money you have women."

"You should put that in your formula."

"Yes, yes, that's the kind I want, formula women—they all prefer money to no money."

Scotty keeps an eye on things and at about three o'clock floats out to assess the afternoon's advances. He totters around, glaring at the turf as if searching for a lost coin. "You missed some," he grunts, pointing at a few blades of wayward greenery. He grabs the clippers. "Like this!" he says, and he humps forward, muttering invective, stabbing at the grass, tearing up bits of sod—eventually having to accept that the clippers are dull, the grass elusive, his resolve spongy, alcohol mightier than duty; and he drops the clippers and turns unsteadily in the direction of his office where, if he can stay upright and put one foot in front of the other over a distance of maybe fifty yards, he can get to his ugly little car and hence to his ugly little office, where he can booze out the day in the luxuriating harmony of the Peaceable Kingdom.

"Sharpen 'em!" he yells over his shoulder, and goes prattling off about how much good university ever did me, ever did anyone, how many millionaires, etc....

Scotty is barely out of sight when we are joined by our sometime clipping companion, Norman, who is seventeen and plays guitar in a rock band in Downsview. He has a kind of sautéed sheen about his face—greasy hair, faint moustache, always has a little garden of pimples blooming around his chin. During his first couple of days at the cemetery he wore a T-shirt bearing the terse directive "Eat shit!" The message was printed in narrow rainbow technoscript about two inches high, and initially Scotty ignored it or was too drunk to notice. But at lunch hour the second day, while Norman was standing in the shop, Scotty inched toward him, bent at the waist, stopping a foot or so in front of Norman's chest, squinting at the multicoloured command.

"Eat *what?*" he said, drawing himself up to look Norman in the eye.

"You know," shrugged Norman, "Eat *stuff!* It's just a T-shirt."

"What sort of stuff?" persisted Scotty, returning his gaze to chest level.

"Stuff!" stammered Norman, "—stuff that, you know, comes out your rear end."

"*Out yer rear end,*" whispered Scotty, straightening up, staring into Norman's face. "Well, son," he said in a soft rolling burr, "arrround here, we don't eat stuff that comes *out yer rear end,* and neither do our berrreaved guests. And to prrreserve us from even having to consider eating stuff that comes *out yer rear end,* I want that T-shirt off these prrremises not in ten seconds or five seconds but before the counting of seconds even has a chance to begin. And if it's not, you'll be off these prrremises yourself—for good. Do you understand, son?"

"I understand," said Norman, protesting nevertheless that with no shirt he would get a sunburn.

Speaking not a word, Scotty retreated upstairs, reappearing momentarily with a filthy old Argyle cardigan held at arm's length between thumb and forefinger. "Here," he said gaily, "put it on," and he watched as Norman slipped into the disgusting garment and pushed its single remaining button through its hole.

"This better not be off a dead guy," Norman said as we left the shop, to which Hogjaw responded that "no self-respecting dead guy would be caught wearing a moth-eaten cardigan with one button," and that Norman himself was "undoubtedly the first cadaver to put the thing on."

Norman's conversation varies but is more often than not a litany of tweeters, wa-was, amplifiers, Ludwigs and Telecasters. Luccio can't stand him and one day tells him, "Rock music's shit, Norman. I don't know how you listen to it."

"Your trouble," Norman responds, "is that you don't know what to listen *for*. You've gotta train your ear."

"To do what?"

"To *listen*, man. To listen to the music. What music do you listen to?"

"Classical," barks Luccio. "Suppositorski."

Beyond his desultory physical labours, Norman's chief contribution to life at the cemetery is the occasional zinger of a story. Like the time he was walking home from a drugstore in Scarborough with a plastic shopping bag when a car squealed up in front of him, blocking his path on the sidewalk. "Coupl'a zit-heads in baseball jackets jump out and push me up against a building and flash their little badges and start shouting they're the police and don't move and get my ID out, all this. So I says I haven't got it with me, and one of 'em says, 'Where ya goin?'"

'Home.'

'What's in the bag?'

'Bumwad,' I tell 'im, and he gets pissed and says, 'Open it up,' and I get pissed cause I haven't done dick. I says, 'How come?' and he says, 'Open it or we'll take ya in for a warrant.'

'Take me in,' I says. So they take me over to the baconbarn on Morningside and they put me in this little room with my bag, and I sit there for two hours, and I know they're watchin me cause there's this little window in the wall, right? And all this time the only thing I'm thinkin is how pissed my old man's gonna be cause he sent me for arsewipe cause he's gotta go and there's none in the house and this is two hours ago, right? So I walk out and I says to the guy at the desk, 'Can I phone my old man?' And he says, 'Get back in there!' And they *lock the door* this time. And after a while two other guys come in, and these new dozers figure they've got some big needlejammer or something. And they show me this piece of paper and say, 'Give us the bag, son—hand it over.' So I do and they open it and pull out a four-pack of arsewipe, and they stand there *starin* at it and *feelin* it and lookin back in the bag. They leave me there, and about an hour later one of 'em comes back and he's gonna drive me home and I says 'Where's my bag, sir?' and he says, 'I assume it's between your legs where everybody else's is,' and I say, 'That's not funny, sir,' and he says, 'We're keeping it till tomorrow.' *They're arresting my arsewipe!* When I get home my old man's fried cause I haven't got the stuff and it's midnight and he had to use newspaper or something. Course he doesn't believe me about the cops till the next day when a cop shows up at the door and hands him the arsewipe and says, 'I hope we didn't cause any inconvenience, sir,' and my old man hollers, 'Not unless you call draggin the *Toronto Star* across your slot an inconvenience! Why didn't you just keep Norman and send me my toilet paper?'"

What really irks Luccio about Norman is not his stories or music or anything of the sort, but his women, or at least his talk of them. Norman claims to have four or five on the string, tends to them like a trapline when he's not practising with his band, which he says is on the verge of a recording contract for an album of songs they intend to start writing any day now. Luccio doesn't see that a pimply teenager has any right to be getting laid when he's not. Especially on four or five fronts.

Then one morning in mid-July Luccio himself walks into work dripping smugness and can't get me aside fast enough to tell me that he himself has bedded a real live woman, one with eyes and lips and flesh-covered limbs and a genuine functioning pelvis—in short, a miracle woman, a friend of his sister's, an academic of some sort, in town from Montreal.

The next afternoon she and the sister drive into the cemetery in the friend's car to pick up Luccio. He wants me to meet them, and as we approach the vehicle I'm impressed to see a pair of fetching Italians with wide smiles and big white teeth. They appear to be in their early thirties. Like Luccio, the friend has a literary bent and is immediately abuzz about the graveyard as a literary item. We're all attention, made for metaphor, pitching in with a yard or two of polysyllabic foolishness of our own.

We work it out that I'll meet them downtown for dinner, which turns out to be a gassy affair with a lot of cheap wine and hyper conversation. Luccio's friend is a talker, a sociologist, a sworn enemy of U.S. foreign policy, the war in Vietnam, rentier capitalism, bourgeois this and that. The drunker she gets the more she dominates the table, bantering politics, culture, philosophy, declaring at one point (more or less silencing the restaurant) that if "Sartre had read Kierkegaard, he'd never have written a gawdam word!"

"How so?" says Luccio softly.

"He'd have realized that flesh and spirit are not inextricably tied!"

Luccio takes a long pull on a bottle of beer. "Knock, knock," he says to no one in particular.

"Who's there?" she says solemnly, but before Luccio can complete the joke his guts erupt in a resounding burp that goes through several increments of pitch before arresting itself in a gurgling snap at the back of his throat. "Excuse me," he whispers and slips off to the washroom, reappearing minutes later with a plate-sized water stain across the front of his shirt.

When the meal is over they all want to go to the Colonial to see Sonny Rollins. Then Lucy, Luccio's sister, decides she'd rather go home, and I'm quick into the breach with the offer of a ride.

As we walk to the car, she asks me about working with Luccio. She volunteers that she doesn't think he'd have lasted at the cemetery if it weren't for me.

Given my affection for him, the remark is both reassuring and flattering, and it catches me off guard. She proceeds to describe how during December and January Luccio would be off to work before daylight, would collapse into bed when he got home, and otherwise never left the apartment except on trips to the library. "He reads more books in a week," she says, "than I read in half a year!"

We clatter along King Street, in and out of the streetcar tracks, go roaring up the Don Valley Parkway, and in no time are sitting in front of a late-forties three-storey walk-up in North York. "What you have to understand about Luccio," she says, "is that he's very proud and very stubborn. He'd never work in a cemetery back home." The catch is that he's also too proud to be broke—or to go home without making something of himself in the wide world.

I ask about the job at Imperial, and she tells me he sent out twenty-seven résumés between Christmas and Easter. "I addressed every one of them," she says. "He gets the interviews, but not the jobs—something about him puts these people off."

While I hesitate to say so, I know exactly what that something is: Luccio is too big, too bright, too confident, too loud—simply too large for the confinements of the corporate office. And the people who might hire him can smell it on him the moment he comes through the door. In an impractical literary sense, he's perfect for the work he's doing. Unfortunately, even the most artful suitability to gravedigging is of limited advantage in what Luccio refers to as "the world of the double-breasted ulcer."

To make a point, I tell her briefly about the world in which I grew up—repressive Baptist fundamentalism—a world in which fear and conformity and a gruelling accountability to God were the inner governor on everything from brainwaves to socializing to the stirring of hormones in the blood. While I am not quite sure how to put it into words, I attempt to tell her how much Luccio has meant to me as a kind of liberating figure, what with his skepticism and intelligence and audacity.

"Now if he can just liberate himself," she laughs. "He likes you, too."

"How old is Luccio?" it occurs to me to ask.

"Thirty-three."

She looks at me squarely and says, "How old are you?"

"Nineteen."

"Nineteen," she nods. "Do you have a girlfriend, Charles?"

Unsure of the preferred answer, I go with the unvarnished truth—not at the moment.

"Has Luccio told you how old I am?"

"No," I lie.

"How old do you think I am?"

"Twenty-five," I tell her.

"That's so nice," she whispers.

Around us, the night has turned cool. A crisp quarter moon hangs like a flaying knife above Avenue Road.

As she is about to get out, she leans over and gives me a gentle kiss on the cheek—a kiss at once stirring, affectionate, cavalier, patronizing, dismissive. She pats me on the knee, a gesture I promptly return, resisting a fierce temptation to slide my hand upward along her thigh.

"Come for dinner sometime," she smiles as she closes the car door.

I tell her to invite me, and within minutes am tearing along the 401, fantasies brimming, galvanized brain astir.

three

THE UNASSAILABLE CODE
OF CEMETERY CONDUCT

THE FOLLOWING morning I am joined in my grass clipping by a couple of Newfoundlanders, brothers, who have "stopped-in-by-chance," as Peter puts it, and gotten hired on probation. Probation is an irresistible concept to Scotty (he pronounces the word as if it had three or four *r*s). If he finds a superior worker he can keep him on. If not, he has the gustatory pleasure of chewing him out, humiliating him as deeply as possible, and then firing him—preferably in front of the other workers. On the contrary, the employee, fired and unfettered, gets the unique opportunity to tell Scotty to his face exactly what he thinks of him—a reversal undoubtedly as stimulating to the old man as is any other part of his twisted probationary procedure.

Before any new employee begins work he must be primed of course. This includes a rare invitation to Scotty's upstairs office, an airless little closet crammed with a half-century's accumulation of mortuary and graveyard supply catalogues, *True Crime* magazines, heaps of old plot maps, generations of stinking work clothes (overalls, toques, long johns); a radio; a bird's nest; a

bucket of coffin nails from the days before coffins were fitted
with latches and pre-installed screws; the grimacing skull of
what appears to have been a dog. On the windowsill sits a scat-
tering of stray bones that may or may not be human and a pair
of topless cremation urns, one bearing lumps of yellowish ash,
the other a set of mouldy false teeth and a 1951 Cadillac Dinky
Toy hearse with "functional coffin cartage." Beyond these, atop
the radiator, stretches a row of eighty-ounce pickle jars containing granite cleaner, rat poison, grave disinfectant, cockroach
bait . . . a decade's supply of industrial-sized Catelli alphabet
noodles, which is to say big seriffed letters used to create the
inscriptions on the lids of the concrete outer vaults before they
get their dignifying coat of "heat-resistant aluminum engine and
chimney paint." (Luccio points out with restrained irony that
the paint might more significantly be applied to the stiffs themselves, the better to protect them on their inevitable arrival in
"the furnace of fire," as their destination has been described by
no less a guide to the hereafter than St. John the Divine.)

On the wall behind Scotty's desk hangs a panoramic photo of
Willowlawn during the Second World War, an era when every
vacant plot was plowed into a Victory Garden—and the dead,
as Peter puts it, "rose atom by atom," reincarnated as string
beans and zucchinis. Beyond that hangs a photo of a wooded
Glasgow churchyard, and beyond that, nailed to the wall, a flattened cardboard box bearing a likeness of what appears to be a
woman's girdle but which is described in 36-point Baskerville
as a "Left-side abdominal truss for non-surgical control of the
herniated bowel."

It is here amidst the desultory rubble of his career that
Scotty delivers to the newcomers his unassailable code of
cemetery conduct: "We-stairt-at-eight-o'clock-around-here-
not-ten-after-not-fave-after, from-eight-in-the-marrning-
to-fave-in-the-afternewn-I-demand-turtle-concentration-

on-warrk, if-a-funeral-comes-in-get-the-hell-outta-the-way,
I-won't-tolerate-any-interference-with-the-bereaved, if-ya-
finish-a-job-don't-sit-on-yer-airse-come-and-ask-me-
fer-another, if-I'm-not-around-ya-trim-grass-around-
the-stewnes-they-always-need-it, I-allow-fave-minutes-
a-day-in-the-shithouse-that's-all, no-jairking-off-it-debases-
the-integrity-of-the-consecrated-ground-if-I-hafta-reprimand-
ya-I-mark-it-down, three-times-and-it's-the-sack, all-ya-
hafta-do-to-get-along-with-me-is-remember-one-thing-I'm-
the-boss-not-the-Wop-not-the-Dutchman-or-anybody-else,
if-ya-take-things-into-your-own-hands-you're-on-your-way,
we-pay-every-second-Fraiday, yer-pay's-2rg-under-the-union-
agraiment, now-get-the-hell-out-there-and-get-to-wark."

FOR THE first couple of hours the brothers are feverishly ener-
getic, bounding around, chattering about their big plans for the
city—the women, the drinking, the apartment. They want to
know how fast I figure they can get to be full gravediggers, into
the bigger money and all. "How much do you make?" one of
them asks.

"About a nickel more than you."

He nods soberly, his assumption confirmed that the big
money lies just around the corner.

But their enthusiasm is mostly talk, and by late morning
the malaise of the place has gotten to them and they've begun
to goof off. One of them goes to sleep at lunch and it takes the
other the better part of thirty seconds, prodding and jostling
him, just to get him to open his eyes. "Work don't appeal to
'im," he says, grinning at several of us, including Norman, who
is respectfully impressed to encounter people even less inclined
than he to grunt labour.

On the way out to Apostles I ask the brothers what part of
Newfoundland they're from. One says Corner Brook, the other

the name of some obscure fishing port, Lapstrake Tongue or something. "It's *nare* Karnerbrook," says the first.

"It's *nowhere* nare Karnerbrook."

"It *is* nare Karnerbrook!"

"It ain't!"

"Bullshitter!"

"You call me a bullshitter, I'll tear your face off."

"I just called you one—tear it off! C'mon, tear it off, tear my face off, I *want* you to tear it off."

"Don't make me, John."

"C'mon, do it, I *want* you to do it!"

The argument flares and fades until neither of them has the energy to sustain it, and we get into the afternoon's work, repairing "sinkers," old graves whose wooden rough boxes and contents have rotted over the years and caved in, leaving a four- or five-inch (or, occasionally, deeper) concavity in the lawn. Sinkers can appear gradually or quite suddenly after heavy rain, the weight of extra water in the soil simply driving everything down. Peter tells me he was once standing on a grave when it dropped. He also tells me about a man and wife, buried side by side, whose graves collapsed at the same moment, though they were buried ten years apart. For repairs you peel back the sod, add topsoil and put the sod back in place. But even with this simple task there are right and wrong manoeuvres, upon which Scotty loves to expound: *For a fave-inch sinker you add not fave inches but SIX inches of soil, understand, boy, SIX inches so that when the soil settles you're dead level and get no complaints, understand?*

The brothers approach the work with competitive ferocity, tearing the first couple of graves into a hogswallow of divots, then lumping up the soil in such a way that they have to bang away with shovels to level the reinstalled sod.

By the middle of the next day Scotty has hounded them so relentlessly they've quit without drawing any pay, leaving

Scotty with tasty new meat for his insatiable bigotry. "Gawdam Newfie fishermen," he mutters as we come in at quitting time. "Waste of a good pink slip. Worrrse than the Wops!" he says loudly so Luccio will hear.

"The Wops have produced the greatest art in the world!" shouts Luccio.

"And how much of it did *you* prrroduce?"

"What have the Scotch done lately?"

"Scotch is a *drrrrink,* ya prrrick!"

Within seconds Luccio has punched his time card and is out the door on his way. But Scotty cannot leave it alone and follows him out shouting, "Name me the rrrivers of Canada! Go on, name them! Name me the rivers! C'mon, name the rivers! . . . Mackenzie! . . . Frrraser! . . . Thompson! . . . Selkirrrk! . . . All Scotsmen, because the Scots opened this gawdam country up and did more for it than anybody including the English, *especially* the English. Name me the first prime minister! Go on, ya prrrick!"

By now Luccio is vaulting across the lawn toward the bus stop, Scotty shouting futilely behind him, then falling silent, standing for a moment, and turning slowly toward the shop, his brain torn somewhere between his ignorant Glaswegian pride and a hundred other torments of his alcoholic existence.

As I leave the shop he says to me in a voice that comes not so much from his voice box as from the gravelly recesses below, "That boy ain't gonna last around here; ya get them clippers sharpened?"

"First thing in the morning," I tell him, but the answer is lost on him, as he's already on his way up the stairs, baggy pants flapping, grey fedora pulled low on his forehead. He glares down briefly through the little rat sunglasses he always wears in the afternoon, disappears into his office, reappears, says, "Ya get them clippers sharpened?"

"Tomorrow," I insist.

Scotty's grandson David, who is cleaning up the shop, smiles at me half-apologetically. David is sixteen, shy, and constantly caught between his obligatory allegiance to his grandfather, without whom he wouldn't have a job, and his allegiance to the other employees, with whom he spends most of his work time and whom he likes. He's so frightened of his grandfather that, once when he'd knocked over a little spirea bush with the tractor, he came to me, tears in his eyes, pleading that I tell Scotty I'd done it, which I did, touching off a predictable explosion of profanity.

David is a willing source of information, and one day tells me about his grandmother, Scotty's wife, who lies home all day in bed, dying of some catastrophic disease for which he doesn't know the name. "Something to do with her kidneys," he supposes. She is Scotty's partner of fifty years, the two of them having come from Glasgow as bride and groom during the 1920s, brimming with optimism for the New World. Now Scotty drives home at noon to heat soup for her and make sad little bird meals and tend to her catheter. In the evening they watch television and read the *National Enquirer* and *News of the World* . . . and eventually make their escapes, she into the land of little green pills, he on the good ship Cutty Sark.

Scotty himself says little about his life, except for occasional references to his early years at the cemetery, when he dug graves with a pick and shovel, brutal work that he exults in recalling, comparing it with contempt to our own puffball labours. Naturally nobody pays any attention till one day in early June when, after two or three days of rain, the entire cemetery is so sodden that the backhoe can't be driven into the Garden of the Blessed Redeemer without cutting eight-inch ruts in the turf. At 8 A.M. sharp Scotty descends the stairs in his sunglasses and lugubrious black raincoat to announce that we're going to have to dig a grave by hand. He is ecstatic. Since Luccio and I are non-union and unlikely to raise a stink over slave labour we are assigned the job.

In rubber boots and the bright yellow raincoats issued by the cemetery we choose an assortment of digging implements, pile them in a wheelbarrow and slouch off in the rain to locate the plot. That done, we retire to a grove of crabapple trees where Luccio rolls a fiery little pre-sacramental to properly prepare us for the work.

We fritter our way through half an hour of unproductivity before things begin to get serious and we run into a succession of rocks and roots, which we have to heave and hack, mud and sweat flying; and by ten o'clock we're all of eighteen inches into the ground. The wet earth is as heavy as potter's clay. Scotty appears, aghast at the Bohemian pace of our labours. He and Luccio dissolve into mutually hateful abuse, which culminates with Luccio demanding that Scotty assign us some help.

"I'll send Fred," Scotty sniffs.

"Fred!" cries Luccio. "What good's Fred?"

"He can keep the place clean, sweep it up."

"We need a *digger*, not a janitor! Give us Norman!"

"Norman who?"

"Norman!" yells Luccio. "He's been here six weeks! You hired him!"

"Ya ya, he's busy. He's no good anyway."

"He can dig!" hollers Luccio.

Twenty minutes later Fred and Norman both show up, Norman wearing a little round welder's hat that accentuates his resemblance to a rodent. Fred looks like an old lady and, for once, isn't at all enthusiastic about work. He has a knot the size of a five-pin ball tied in the free arm of his raincoat.

"So whaddaya want us to do?" says Norman.

"Oh, just stand there," says Luccio. "Too bad you don't have your guitar—*get a shovel for krisakes!*"

Since there's only so much room in the grave, we work out a system whereby each of us takes a turn digging furiously for three or four minutes, until our arms and shoulders won't function, then crawling out and letting the next man in. While he's not digging, Norman lurches back and forth, eyes closed, solemnly miming Peter Townsend or Keith Richards or whatever other guitarist happens to be on his brain. Fred fusses with a broom for a few minutes and disappears into the mists.

By the time we're four feet down we've caught up with the swollen water table and are actually digging under water. Scotty comes out just before lunch and is enraged to see a foot of muddy slop in the bottom of the grave. But his wrath turns quickly to pragmatism, intense consideration of the problem. Unlike most of his inflated woes, this is serious. For one thing, it is against the law to bury a corpse under water. Scotty's respect for the law, though, is small compared to his fear that a waterlogged grave—a "slurpee" in the lingo of the trade—could be bad for business. Word could get around. More immediately, there is the problem of the mourners, who will be arriving shortly, and will be anything but comforted to see their beloved lowered into a hundred-odd gallons of cocoa-brown swill.

"The *pump*," grunts Scotty, "the *pump*—we'll use the *pump*." He keeps an ancient Briggs & Stratton gas-powered water pump, a sputtering antique contraption, beneath the stairs to his office. It is one of his fondest possessions, and he has maintained it obsessively for nearly four decades—tuned it and polished it and oiled it, to the point where it has become for him a kind of fatted calf, to be brought out only for the most significant occasions, such as a potential loss of business.

Peter is summoned and, within minutes, has delivered the senile old thing to the gravesite. A half-dozen tugs on the starter cord produce a few clicks and pops, a promissory belch, then an explosion of blue smoke as the pump roars to life with the fury of an unmuffled road hog. *"Yeeeaaahhh,"* screams Norman, who winces into a contorted riff on his imaginary guitar and goes pitching across the lawn in a Chuck Berry duck walk.

Luccio throws the intake pipe into the grave, and I drag the outlet hose a hundred feet across the grass. Even before I set it down it is puking muddy grey water.

Within minutes the grave is dry, and we are back at our digging. But as usual at the graveyard, one set of problems has been directly succeeded by another. The latest concern is that, to keep the grave dry, the pump, with its billowing effusions, will have to be left running until the funeral arrives after lunch. By that time, the entire west side of the cemetery, a massive topological sump, will be a haze of toxic exhaust. The rain and humidity are keeping the fumes earthbound, and there isn't a puff of wind to carry them away.

By the time we finish the work and trundle off for lunch, a fountain of nausea is rising in my guts and throat. Peter, too, is feeling it. Luccio, in need of a toke post-haste, is off on his own to take the cure.

Because it is near the end of a pay period and none of us has any money, we have foresworn restaurants. In the rain, however, there is nowhere to eat but in the plywood shack where we change into our work clothes. The place has all the charm of prison solitary: one 60-watt bulb, a few battered lockers and, in the middle of the room, a cut-down coffin crate that functions as a table. On the wall beside the door, there is a faded calendar advertising Ferocrete Burial Vaults and showing a fetching brunette attired (the better to endure her bereavement) in a little black apron and no skivvies. The place is as grubby as a litter box but is nonetheless mythologized as the one-time trysting site of a long-departed gravedigger, "Ernest the Furnace," and a middle-aged secretary who is also long gone from the institution. In the corner, on the floor, in faded ballpoint, is the almost calligraphic inscription (sic): "On these unsweeped board Ernest G expeeriance the most hapiast of hapyness with Rosy P"—and on an exposed stud nearby: "The A. Scotty MacKinnon Academy of Erotic Atrocity."

Opening my lunch does nothing to ease my nausea—four peanut butter and banana sandwiches, the bananas pasty, the bread compressed to what Luccio describes as "the consequential density" of communion wafers—"of the precious sacred Host," he says softly, and he launches a dope-inspired improv on the culinary zest that, were he "chief resident of the Vatican," he would impart to the bland and ashen sacraments of antiquity. *"The Host Tartinade!"* he cries. *"The Host Over Easy! . . . Corned Beef on the Host!"*

Fred, meantime, gnaws into a cooking onion and makes a sandwich of fresh pear slices and bacon drippings. He regularly brings a half dozen garlic cloves, pops them into his mouth and chews them up like Smarties.

Hogjaw has his weekly wad of bread pudding. He fondles it in his unwashed hands, plucking off the daintiest of morsels, dipping each into an unlabelled bottle of yellow jam before poking it into his mouth. He washes everything down with cold tea sucked directly from the spout of a battered orange juice carton.

When he is finished eating, Fred disappears into the rain to perform some shadowy task endemic to his shadowy existence. He is a phenomenon, a mole, operating entirely beneath and beyond the issues of the day and of the graveyard—beyond politics, beyond statistics, beyond law; blissfully beyond newspapers and television. He goes about his business attuned only to some mysterious cadence in his head—and of course to his peonies and roses, to when they pollinate and when they bloom, what aids them and what ails them.

Of the Fred stories I have heard, perhaps the best is that he once trained a skunk at Willowlawn so that the animal would not only appear when he whistled for it but would eat sardines, grapes and such, out of his hand. Then the unexpected: a summer morning, a funeral, a coterie of excessively groomed women in little black dresses, their husbands in crow-coloured suits. And a flute solo of all things, a farewell serenade, indistinguishable to the skunk (in its skunk hole nearby) from Fred's own beckoning whistle.

"At least it was wearing black when it showed up," shrugs Peter, who reports that, when the animal wandered out of the bushes into the midst of the burial party the mourners leapt for the territories—all except for the flutist who, committed to her music, eyes soulfully closed, continued to play while the skunk waited patiently for breakfast to appear.

BY THE end of lunch hour, Scotty has devised a signal system that will enable us to pull the pump from the grave at the last possible instant before the funeral arrives. He himself will stand at the front gate to the cemetery, Peter on a hill a hundred yards or so from the grave. At the instant Scotty sees the hearse coming down Kingston Road, he'll wave to Peter, who'll wave to Luccio, who will shut off the pump and drag it out of sight. The plan is explained to us as if it were a complex military manoeuvre that would affect the fate of continents.

When the signal comes, we remove the pump and drag it uphill into the crabapple trees, quickly gathering up the hose. The mourners appear and take their places at graveside, more than a few of them mugging and muttering over the impressive blue smog that surrounds them. In the distance, we can hear their periodic coughs. The entire unhealthy scene, with its diffuse light and uncertain imagery, suggests a Turner seascape.

As the service proceeds, Scotty takes the undertaker aside and warns him that the coffin must not be lowered—absolutely, positively—until after the mourners have gone. There is no question he'll be heeded; Scotty gets far more respect from the undertakers than he gets from his own tatty underlings. Unlike us, they need him, are dependent on him to make sure that graves are dug on time and are properly laid out, and that there's someone waiting at the cemetery gate, usually Scotty himself, to lead their funerals to the proper gravesites—a significant service in a cemetery of more than thirty thousand graves. In return for Scotty's attentions, the undertakers reimburse him at Christmas by discreetly delivering to the cemetery case upon case of his particular brand of high-octane psycho-damage-control potion, Cutty Sark Scotch Whisky. Twenty-odd cases of it a year roll in, one from each of the funeral homes on the east side of the city—Cutty Sark and Cutty Sark only. Apparently, a few years earlier a young undertaker from an upstart funeral home delivered a festively wrapped case of some other brand of Scotch to the cemetery on Christmas Eve. Before he'd handed over his tariff or had said even as much as Merry Christmas, Scotty espied some slight irregularity in the dimensions of the carton and ordered the young man back to the liquor store for the preferred sap.

As always, when the mourners are safely in their cars and on their way, we return to the grave and unlatch the lowering frame. The coffin descends smoothly for a couple of feet and comes bobbing to rest, gently afloat on the rising tide of groundwater.

We reactivate the pump, and in no time the coffin is solidly on bottom.

"Fill it in!" yells Scotty, as he totters across the lawn toward the grave. "It's not gonna fill itself!"

Luccio takes a couple of steps toward him and says softly, "That's an untenable philosophic assumption, Scotty—it's unworthy of you. Just because no other grave has ever filled itself doesn't mean this one won't. The laws of science and nature are empirical but by no means inviolate."

Scotty stops two feet in front of him, glaring at him as if at an escaped gorilla.

"The only way we can test the assumption," Luccio tells him, "is to leave the grave open and *see* if it fills itself. At this point we have no hard evidence that it won't."

Scotty teeters momentarily and a curtain of malice descends over his face. "When you write your will," he sputters, "put it down that you'd like precisely that assumption tested on *your* grave. In the meantime, get this one filled in or you've got your pink slip."

Well pleased with his rejoinder, he slouches off in the direction of the crabapple trees, homing in on his beloved water pump.

AT THE shop, the snack truck has arrived. In response to my dope-aroused cravings, I order a large coffee, a cinnamon bun and a couple of Niagara peaches. Luccio orders two cokes and an Eat-More bar, and then a second Eat-More and a bag of peanuts.

My banquet consumed, I remove my T-shirt and stretch out along the shop wall where a little puddle of sunlight has found its way through the clouds. The combination of exhaustion and dope induces sleep and an almost instantaneous dream. Like many of my dreams lately, this one is set in the cemetery and is animated by an array of rubbery mourners, one of whom seems to be myself. Fred glides into our midst, aged and shirt-less, revealing a vivid purple chest boil, perhaps a nipple, from which he squeezes with great effort: a beetle, a stone, a piece of overripe fruit . . . and (for his grand finale) the oily black fist of his rediscovered arm.

four

A YOUNG MAN OF SPIRITUAL
INCLINATIONS

FOR THOSE of you who missed it, or have forgotten, 1969 was, among other things, a time of flower children, free love, campus protest, the battle for civil rights, the death of God.

The Beatles, the best known pop band in history, were nearing the end of their mercurial sojourn, and a hamburger chain that would eventually dominate the fast-food industry was just beginning its mission to spread trans-homicidal fats to the unsuspecting patty-eaters of the world.

In mid-August of that year, while I was busy painting burial vaults and lowering corpses, half a million people gathered on six hundred acres of pastureland in Bethel, New York, and held a rock festival named for a town forty miles upwind, the latter now a metaphor both for the era and for the era's inhabitants, the so-called "Woodstock generation."

That same summer, a pair of U.S. astronauts climbed down the ladder of their coleopteran spacecraft, planted an American flag on the moon, and, of all things, knocked a golf ball around amid the rocks and moon dust, in the reduced gravitational pull.

Years later, Timothy Leary, the Acid King, would web-
cast the hours leading up to his death to the hip world of his
admirers. But at the time, death was still singularly unhip—as
was burial in the days before designer and biodegradable coffins. When Jack Kerouac, one of the icons of the hip generation died spitting blood that year at the age of forty-seven, they
dressed him in a fifty-dollar suit (no beads), stuck him in a two-
hundred-dollar box and, having delivered his soul prayerfully
unto the ages, dropped his booze-swollen corpse into the unhip
ground in his hometown of Lowell, Massachusetts. It was all so
desperately square, so out of cadence with the spirit of the age
and of the man that, according to the poet Gregory Corso, who
was there, Kerouac's friends (the lot of them jacked up on bour-
bon) considered yanking him from his coffin as he lay in the
funeral parlour in Lowell and dragging him down to the bar for
last call.

For me, at university, the prevalent issue was the war in Vietnam, a pointless and much-protested conflagration in which the
world's wealthiest nation was literally scorching the daylights
out of one of the world's poorest—spraying napalm gel onto
defenceless villagers, leaving them screaming and aflame, and
spraying a carcinogenic defoliant named Agent Orange onto
anything else that looked like it might pose an impediment to
the spread of global peace. Coincidentally, at Willowlawn, we
used a diluted form of that same Agent Orange in the less hostile
but equally pointless war against plantain and dandelions.

In the West, the Cold War shivered on, its main argument
seemingly arising over which of the world's "superpowers,"
with their apparently divergent philosophies, was best suited to
controlling the planet: the one that kicked the bejeesus out of
poor and vulnerable countries for political and economic advantage or the one that kicked the bejeesus out of poor and vulnerable countries for political and economic advantage.

On a more positive note, young women (as the song says) were wearing flowers in their hair, and very short skirts and no bras. Panty girdles, which had dominated their loins for a decade and, like death, had no natural place in the dream state that was Aquarius, had given way to panties, and then to no panties—and just in time. One of my fondest memories of 1969 (whose numerical dub, it hardly needs saying, was a sexual insinuation unto itself) was being led by my lab partner into the deserted greenhouse of the University of Toronto botany building, to a remote and jungle-like corner, where she leaned over a seedling table, flipped up her kilt, exposing her panty-less bottom and invited me (in the argot of the era) to do my thing—which, under the circumstances, I did with poodle-like enthusiasm.

AS TO how I came to be working in the unlikely Stygian rat-hole that was Willowlawn Everlasting, it wasn't difficult. At the time, I was a second-year student in science and philosophy at the University of Toronto. I had finished my exams in mid-April, was in a state of financial dysfunction to rival that of my name-sake, Wilkins Micawber, and desperately needed a job.

Unfortunately, none was available—at least none for a nineteen-year-old cloud-gazer whose employment record consisted of three summers as a canoeing instructor at a Kawartha-area girls camp and occasional winter forays into "clinical testing" for products that, among others, included Bradley's Nova Blemish Erase (a pork-chop-coloured pimple application that under black light, I discovered the hard way, turned the skin a bruisy irides-cent purple).

By the first of May, I had been turned down by a dozen potential employers, among them Shubang Used Tire on Jarvis Street and Dick's Nifty Car Wash on Danforth Avenue—had in fact become so hopeless of landing a job that every night I had to convince myself again that somewhere there was a standard of employment meaningless enough for me.

My parents, lifelong evangelical Christians, believed that Bible college and what they invariably referred to as "the mission field" might be a suitable choice for a young man of spiritual inclinations. What I could not tell them, and never did, was that my faith at that point was the proverbial burned-out house—a reality perhaps best represented by the fact that a year or so earlier I had hollowed out the pages of my baptismal Bible and was using it for, among other things, condom storage (my first safe deposit box) and for the secure keeping of my supply of marijuana and rolling papers. Instead, I told them that I simply wasn't cut out to be a missionary, hesitating to add that in all the years of my biblical indoctrination, my only interest in missions had come as a twelve-year-old when it struck me with considerable force that life in Africa would at least be brightened by exposure to half-naked black women of the sort I had seen in *National Geographic*—women, that is, whose mahogany-coloured breasts resembled a fusion of my mother's drawstring handbag and the extraordinary gourds that my father grew in his garden and, at Thanksgiving, piled on the altar at Brimstone Baptist Church.

One evening as I sifted the classifieds for the third or fourth time, my eye settled on an ad calling for encyclopedia salesmen, which I had glimpsed other days but had strategically ignored. The following morning, I arranged an interview that, happily, I never got to. As I sped across the eastern suburbs of the city, I passed an enormous wooded cemetery. On an impulse of combined curiosity and self-preservation, I cut across traffic and wheeled in through the wrought-iron gates.

Two mornings later at 7:15, the phone rang in my parents' apartment, where I was living for the summer. My father, who at that point knew nothing of the graveyard, took the call and, with shaving cream on his benignly weary face, padded down the hall to my room and nudged me on the shoulder. "Somebody called Scotty says you're to be at the marble farm in forty-five minutes," he said softly. "You'd better get moving . . . Don't fall in!" he called as he padded out of the room and back down the hall.

An hour later, Scotty (who took no pains to hide a suspicion that, in me, he had hired decidedly the wrong bone-waxer) gave me a ten-second rundown on the mores of the cemetery and sent me off pronto to the Garden of Eternal Remembrance to find "the Wop" whom I was to assist until coffee break.

"Remembrance," I quickly learned, was a tract of military graves, most of them marked by simple stone crosses. But after ten minutes of strolling among the markers, glancing at the inscriptions, I had found no one. I walked to the top of a gentle rise and boosted myself onto the base of a bronze soldier from where I could see out across the terrain. Weeks later, during a burial, it would occur to me in a modest satori that these graves belonged not to men who were remembered for their military heroics, if there had been any, but who had survived their wars and died at home as retired salesmen, office managers, deracinated husbands. No wonder, I thought, it was as gunners, tank drivers, bombers—as fighting men—that they had chosen to be remembered to the world.

I was on the point of returning to the shop when the shambling figure of a man materialized out of the haze in a neighbouring section of the graveyard. As he approached, I could see cradled along his forearm three polished wooden boxes, ornate little caskets, containing, I would learn, cremated human remains. In his other hand he held a bright orange posthole digger. A book whose title I couldn't see was tucked into his pants. He greeted me cheerfully, introduced himself as Luccio and tossed the boxes to the ground.

Each of the thirty thousand plots at Willowlawn is marked by an identifying cornerstone, and within minutes we were snooping around, our noses at belt level, searching for the bits of blue-chip real estate in which we were to bury the containers.

· When we had located the first of them, Luccio dug a knee-deep hole and said, "Throw me one of those birdhouses."

"Which one?" I said, examining them on the ground.

"Any of them."

I looked at him, thinking I had misunderstood.

"It doesn't matter," he said. "They're all the same."

I stood immobilized as he walked over to the boxes, winked at me and picked one up. He'd been doing this for a year, he deadpanned, and hadn't had a complaint.

"By the way," he said, holding up the rococo little bone crypt, with its crenellated eaves and shiny brass top, "How would you like to spend eternity rammed into this piece of shit?"

An hour later, I followed him to a grove of ornamental cedars where he pulled a tiny plastic bag from his shirt pocket.

"There are two things you have to do to survive around here," he told me as he twisted a bud of shredded marijuana into a rolling paper. "The first is to pay no attention whatever to anybody in any position of authority—that's crucial. The second is to spend as little time as possible thinking about reality. This helps," he said, and, touching a match to the tip of the reefer, he took a first long pull on it, and then another—and, with the deftness of the well-practised teahead, handed it to me.

AFTER COFFEE break of that first morning on the job, I was sent out to the Garden of the Old Testament Patriarchs to trim grass around the stones. By 11 A.M., in eighty degrees of heat, I had abandoned my shirt. By 2 P.M., I felt the first inklings of the sun crab on my back, and by four o'clock was as badly sunburned as I have ever been. At 4:30 I helped Luccio mark out a grave for the next morning and, an hour later, was flat on my stomach, in my parents' apartment, moaning quietly with each exhaled breath. For several insufferable seconds, against my agonized grunts, my mother applied Solarcaine to skin that, by this time, was the colour of Barbie doll packaging and, by Wednesday, would be the texture of bubble wrap. On Tuesday morning, I phoned Scotty at 7:45 and explained to him with apologies that, for this day at least, I was unfit for the digging or tending of graves.

"I thought you said you was a good worker!" he responded with singsong cruelty.

"I am," I told him. "But I'm in too much pain."

"One day on, one day off," he said. And with a sarcastic chuckle he hung up the phone.

I went back to lying on my stomach, part of me thinking less repugnantly about a start in encyclopedia sales—or, indeed, on the mission field—a more resilient part thinking that I would show this bile-spewing piece of highland sheep shit, this officious prick, that I was made of tough enough hide and gristle not just to survive but to thrive amidst the withering exigencies of the graveyard.

As indeed I turned out to be, insinuating myself into Willowlawn's version of *la danse macabre* with the diligent attention of a bluebottle on a roadside stiff.

five

THE PRACTICE

OF INEFFICIENCY

BY THE TIME we finish filling the hand-dug grave, only an hour of the work day remains. Since it is too wet to trim stones or cut grass, and since none of us is in a mood to start anything new, we must do our best to look busy or to stay out of sight. I push a barrow-load of implements up to the shop, dump them on the driveway and spend the next half hour scraping them to the metal and then washing them in the sink so that they gleam like cooking utensils.

A squalid little outhouse stands beside the repair shop, half hidden by cedars. The exterior of the place is neatly painted and trimmed, all very discreet, right down to the ornate Celtic cross cut in the door. The interior, however, is a revolting gallery of smells and graffiti, the latter aimed mostly at Scotty, wishing him quartered, castrated, eviscerated. It is one of the hazards of the institution that the biffy's seat planks aren't properly joined and that the fractional space between them can put a nasty little ferret bite on the backside of an unsuspecting visitor. The pit of horrors below is prevented from being an all-out obscenity only

by the occasional application of MistoVan (a commodity dis-
pensed by Scotty in one of dozens of miniature tin cans saved
from the days before his blood pressure went supernova and his
preferred morning snack was a kill shot of Cutty and a mini-can
of "saucisse Viennoise"—full-sodium cocktail wieners).

And yet the place has attractions as a sanctuary. A former
employee, "Pirmin the German" (a celebrated reprobate who
five years after his dismissal is still cited by Scotty for his peer-
less sloth), is said to have avoided work for hours by locking
the door behind him, going so far at times as to eat his lunch
inside, making himself comfortable in winter by lighting a can
of Sterno on the seat beside him. The story goes that one day
Scotty happened by and, having smelled the fumes, began banging on the door. When no answer came, he smashed off the
hinges with a twenty-pound tamping iron, firing Pirmin only
after he had forced the fabled minion to repair every splinter of
the damage.

Understandably, for Scotty, the outhouse is an all-but-biblical
symbol of lost time, insubordination and human sneakiness. He
has removed the lock from the door and insists that it be left open
when nobody is inside. He can see just a corner of it from his
office window and can thus assure himself at a glance that nobody
is hiding out on him. Although here, as always, the employees are
a step ahead of him and simply leave the door open when they go
in for a little down time.

Such subterfuges aren't always possible of course. Often
there's simply too much work to do to allow for lingering. At
other times—say, toward the end of lunch hour, when a line-up
can form—whoever happens to be inside is likely to be subjected
to a kind of hazing, a rocking, so that even something as simple
as pissing in a toilet becomes an act of Olympian exactitude.

Needless to say, we could pee outdoors. However, to do so
would consume marginally less work time than using the shitter,

and is thus rigorously avoided by employees for whom the practice of inefficiency is a sort of mystic commitment unto itself.

On this particular afternoon, Scotty has left his copy of the *National Enquirer* on the workbench in the shop. From there, I spirit it to the dumper, where I consume a series of *Enquirer* exclusives, including a late-breaking scoop entitled "Crooked Descendant of Jesus Runs Galilee Carpenters' Union," as well as a half-page feature on the role of ex-Nazis in the California peace movement. The fear among "peace leaders," it seems, is that the likes of Adolf Eichmann, Josef Mengele and Rudolf Hess—all of whom have apparently "taken shelter" as reconstructed hippies hiding out from the Mossad—will turn "hoards of drug-crazed peaceniks" into an American version of the Third Reich.

Presently, there are footsteps on the gravel path, and I jettison the *Enquirer* and attempt to look like a man about his business. However, the alarm is false: It's not Scotty but Luccio. At six-foot-three, 240 pounds, he quite literally darkens the doorway, orders me to shove over and, without dropping his pants, settles onto the board seat beside me. He stares into the little arbour of evergreens beyond the door and whispers, "I can't take it anymore, Wilkins." He shuts his eyes, heaves a guttering sigh. The fact that he has not shaved for several days adds an impressive veil of depravity to his mood and demeanour. He swings his face toward me, opens a malevolent eye and says softly, "But before I quit, my friend, I have a duty to perform in the interest of mankind. It may be the only thing I ever do for purely humanitarian reasons." He has it all worked out and, pausing barely to breathe, he spins out the through-line on a nasty little butcher-shop opera, a Halloween fantasy wherein one day very soon he will have his cohort Peter dig a secret grave; he will hide beneath the shop stairs at quitting time, will ambush the little highlander, will tie him up, will throw him in the front-end loader.

Without bending a note of his sweet, vengeful caprice, Luccio extracts a tiny yellow roach from his shirt pocket, lights it with utmost dexterity and having drained it of its last atom of potency, flicks it between his legs into the sewage pot below. He will "flay the old man's hide," take it off a strip at a time; will blind him with lye, rub salt into his skinless carcass. "And a little lemon juice, Wilkins—you can't beat a little lemon juice in the war against inner filth." Did I know, he demands, that a human being can be kept alive with just ten percent of his skin intact? Under cover of darkness, he will transport the squirming remains to the dug grave; will raise the loading bucket to max height for added splat; will spray the old man with grave disinfectant. In the name of gratuitous torment, he will pour in a bottle of Cutty Sark, making sure not a drop finds the toothless gums, the peeled tongue of his parched tormentor. Now he is on his feet, nearly knocking me from my own narrow half of the two-seater. He glares into the shitter. "I'm so very deeply sorry, Mr. MacKinnon—however, I have no choice but to dismiss you from your life's work as a soulless snippet of arse lint." He brandishes an imaginary pink slip, drops it fluttering into the latrine. He will fill the grave a shovelful at a time—no, no, will fill it with the loader, silencing quickly Scotty's pained and muffled protests; he will drive the old man's Vauxhall to "some bottomless lake"; will sink the thing and be on his way to Italy before anyone knows or cares that Scotty is missing. "It's the perfect crime, Wilkins, the unsolvable murder—*no fucking stiff*," he says. "Who'd ever think to look for a body in a cemetery?"

"Why do you have to go to Italy if it's an unsolvable crime?"

"Ah, Wilkins," he sighs, "you have a brilliant criminal mind—thank you for the insight, you're so right, I needn't run at all. I can stay right here for the rest of my life—no need to interrupt my career; you should be a consultant in these matters, my good man; consultancy pays. I may need your complicity—*but wait,*" he says. He suggests that I may want to dispatch Scotty myself, to do something meaningful with my thus-far irrelevant life. "If you get caught, I'll defend you! I studied law, you'll never hang, Wilkins! If you do, I'll be there for you; I'll cut you down; I'll claim your carcass; I'll bury you myself."

His energy waning, he thumps back onto the seat, fusses in his shirt pocket and produces another roach, this one with sufficient guts to provide both of us a bit of a bracer against the toxins of the shithouse and of the afternoon.

OUTSIDE, THE shadows are lengthening, and as we step into the daylight and cross the road, Peter approaches on the tractor, pulling a wagon bearing the water pump and lowering device, plus a yard or so of wet clay that is the displacement from the grave. Scotty appears out of the shop. "What're you so pleased about?" he quacks at Luccio. "You only did half a day's work!"

"That's half a gawdam day more than you did!" protests Luccio. But before the old man can rise to the bait, Luccio is messing with him, cajoling him, defusing his focus. "Actually, we should all be ecstatic," he says. "Did you hear? I've conceived the perfect crime!"

Something of a devotee of illicit activity himself, Scotty demands to know what the impeccable crime might be.

"Not only am I going to fulfill a long-cherished fantasy and walk away *Scot-free,*" boasts Luccio, "I'm going to rid the planet of one of its most pressing and insidious evils! Unfortunately, you won't be around to enjoy the results, my good man!" At this, he cuts abruptly away from Scotty into the Garden of the Apostles of the Living Christ on a beeline for the change shack.

"Gawdam scholar," mutters Scotty. He turns to me, his sallow smile the thinnest of possible disguises. "What's he gonna do? What's he mean I won't be around? Is he gonna quit?"

THE NEXT morning, in the change shed, it occurs to me to ask Peter why Scotty doesn't simply act on his near-daily inclinations to fire Luccio—to rid the place forever of the contemptuous Italian with his non-stop insubordination.

The truth, according to Peter, is that, with the exception of Fred, the old man would rather fire anybody else on staff, and he explains that despite Scotty's loathing of the aspiring Doctor of Philosophy, he understands well the advantages of having a deployable 240-pound foot soldier on the payroll and is unlikely to tie the can to him over anything as inconsequential as corrosively irresolvable hatred. As Hogjaw puts it, where else for the price of the minimum wage could Scotty find someone with the strength of a rhino to dig holes and drag burial vaults around, and to be on hand should his formidable muscle be needed?

Luccio himself tells me how, on a day last autumn, Scotty came lurching across the Garden of the Holy Blessed Virgin, hollering at him to come quick; a fight had erupted during a high-church interment and things were about to get worse. By the time Luccio got there the mourners and funeral attendants had retreated from the grave into a kind of spectators' circle, and were gazing stupefied as two drunken relatives crashed around the suspended coffin, kicking and throwing roundhouses at one another—a scene brought precipitously to a halt when Luccio grabbed the drunkest of the pair, carried him wriggling to the road and with the funeral director's help shut him in the back of the hearse until the police arrived.

It is not until a day in late June, however, that I myself see Luccio deployed as a muscle cop. There has been a complaint from an irritable old man whose wife is buried in the Garden of the Blessed Redeemer and who has several times encountered what he describes as "a giant wino" who is apparently spending nights in an arbour of old lilacs in the back acres. Bad enough that the blighted colossus should be asnooze in the consecrated preserve, but he is said to have been dozing *well into the mid-morning* (when of course all respectable winos should be productively about their business, accosting straight folk and guzzling eighty-cent Catawba). Scotty, whose perception of the intruder is that of some funeral-crashing Sasquatch and who is fearful for his skin, engages Luccio to accompany him on recon for whatever presumptuous trespasser has encamped prematurely in the land of long fingernails.

For Luccio, the exercise couldn't be more appealing. For one thing he immediately recognizes his own questionable likeness as the sleeping galoot of the old man's complaint and is resigned, at least poetically, to this new phase of the long-time search for himself. To that end, he accompanies Scotty to an obscure corner of Redeemer where the boss is disappointed to discover not his intended quarry but a couple of feckless drifters huddled under a willow with a newspaper and a couple of stubbies of Red Cap.

Having hustled them from their hideaway, Luccio suggests to Scotty that he, Luccio, sequester himself in that part of the cemetery for an hour on the chance that the brazen scofflaw might again show his face. Scotty endorses the idea as a canny bit of security and leaves Luccio to half a day of unmolested reading. At afternoon break, Luccio marches into the shop and, with Scotty and the rest hanging on every phrase, reports that el Diablo has indeed shown up and that he has evicted him with the warning that if ever again he trespasses on the sacred soil, he will be given a shovel and a set of clippers and conscripted into the final mortification, employment at Willowlawn.

six

THE PROFITABLE
PHASE OF DEATH

BEHIND THE brawling and blustering and botched graves—and the day lilies and lilacs—the cemetery is of course a rip-snorting money mill, the lube for which pours out of a grubby second-floor business office behind Scotty's lair. From there, a team of smarmy hirelings on telephones does its best to convince potential customers that they should invest their money in the tiny plots of sod that will eventually house their bones. The options to the customer are endless—dozens of prices in any number of settings in a "full range" of plot configurations: "single," "double," "family," "extended family," as well as the popular and prudent "thrift plot," the "double-decker" or "one-over" as it is known in the trade—a grave in which one coffin can legally be stacked atop another.

The salespeople make as many as a hundred calls a day each—well-rehearsed intrusions that begin invariably with a flurry of false warmth and descend rapidly into the pitiable subterfuge that the telephone companies have promoted and attempted to dignify as "telemarketing."

The object of the phone call is to get into the client's home, preferably into his living room, where the object becomes getting him to visit Willowlawn. Once there, the idea is, simultaneously, to appeal to his sense of self-importance (picture yourself in a prestige plot) and to skewer his sense of guilt over buying anything but the best for his loved ones—in short, to gore him as deeply as possible, sell him the best sun in winter, best shade in summer, best fall colours, best view, finest statuary, quietest surroundings, closest proximity to the rose gardens . . . all of which are but a prelude, of course, to implied amenities such as the Long Soft Landing in Eternity, which, back here on earth, comes invariably with the loftiest of price tags.

Occasionally the pitch produces a backlash, as it did one humid afternoon as Norman and I were trimming graves in the Garden of the Last Supper—"trimming Supper" as Scotty would have it. A young salesman named Owen came quietly up behind us trailing a middle-aged man with a gut as big as a garbage bag and a face iced in permanent hostility. As Owen jabbered away about the view, the lilacs, the shade—"the context" as the sales force calls it—the man planted his feet and with no preamble hollered, "I'M GONNA BE DEAD FER KRISAKES! I WANT A HOLE IN THE GROUND! I WANT THE CHEAPEST GAWDAM HOLE YOU'VE GOT!"

The response sent Owen into grotesque toadying, anything to please, anything not to lose the sale. Could he show Mr. So-and-so something in another garden?

"I TOLD YA I DON'T NEED A GAWDAM GARDEN! I NEED A HOLE IN THE GROUND. I'M GONNA BE DEAD!"

"We'll look in Holy Blessed Virgin," whispered Owen, shooting us a glance of combined disgrace and terror, steering his reluctant mark toward the less desirable neighbourhoods along the outer fences (neighbourhoods where, as Hogjaw puts it, the grass may be a little browner, the soil a little stonier, but the sexual opportunities and rate of unemployment tend to be about the same as anywhere else).

Of all the bedevilling elements of the sales pitch, perhaps the ugliest is the planting of the suspicion that, if left to them, one's relatives and heirs might eschew the expensive and dignified in favour of the cut-rate and chintzy, which is to say the cheap grave, leaving dear old Aunt Bigotty in eternal residence among the homeless, the garlic-eaters, the artists, all the fuck-ups and nonconformists whom she has spent a lifetime scorning for their bad haircuts and seditious opinions and contemptible politics. It is all but a factual conclusion among the salespeople that those committed to the better regions of the marble farm— to the rose gardens, the shade trees, the morose renditions of the (justifiably) weeping Jesus—are statistically better positioned to enter Paradise than are the niggers and nutcases and poets, not to mention the plain old poor, who in their ill-tended plots are almost certainly on a descent into Hell.

And why wouldn't your relatives do such a thing? goes the subtext of the pitch. *Easy way to grab a few extra dollars for themselves!*

Fix 'em before they fix you!

It hardly needs saying that the salespeople are on commission and consider anyone who balks at their inflated prices and claims for eternal prosperity to be of sub-reptilian stinginess, entirely without character or credibility. Those who buy in are of course pampered and spit-waxed until the glow on their cheeks is within a wavelength of the irradiating sheen coming off their wallets and chequebooks. In settling their long-range real estate needs, in laying down the moola, they have been elevated in status from the mere "living" to the illustrious "pre-dead," engaged no longer in what Luccio calls "the sweet grubby vicissitudes of life"—in life's rancour and chaos and potential for unproductivity—but in the introductory, the yet-upright and profitable phase of death.

According to Luccio, it was a belief of the ancient Tibetans that the spirit leaves the body within three days of death (the occurrence marked by the appearance of a drop of pure water from one or another of the mouth, the ear, the nose, the tear duct, the urethra). "In this fucking culture," he says by way of comparison, "the spirit starts leaving the body within three days of birth," coaxed forth and stomped, he believes, by a succession of authoritarian stupidities that begins with baptism, *Romper Room,* the first day of kindergarten—a process eventually finished by the universities and corporations, all the latter-day successors to what he calls "the inquisitional priesthoods of antiquity."

Where repressive and manipulative politics are concerned, he believes that the universities, with their altars and acolytes and incurable internal toxicity, make even the most reactionary of the churches look like a libertarian wife-swapping party.

He knows my own background and is not above a withering condemnation of conservative Christianity—a perspective in which we tend to be aligned. However, it doesn't stop me from arguing that Christianity, like socialism, might work if any culture ever actually tried it.

"But they never will," he says quietly, noting the resistance of most self-respecting societies to organizations run by men in "floor-length black dresses with an appetite for little boys."

I tell him that's not the kind of Christianity I'm talking about, to which he responds that he knows what I'm talking about and that even the "good kind of Christianity is like the good kind of brain cancer."

Later that afternoon, as we poke away at sinkers, he tells me that in parts of southern Italy the poor lease graves, and that seven years is apparently a standard contract, after which the occupant's relatives either pay up (often at an inflated price) or see their loved one pitched into a common grave.

Scotty, who knows more than anybody about the oddities of the global death industry, tells me one day that in Hallstatt, Austria, a twenty-five-hundred-year-old salt-mining town, the mountains come down so precipitously to the shores of the local lake that there is simply no room for permanent burial of the dead. The result is that for hundreds of years, corpses have been kept for exactly twelve years in the town's tiny Catholic cemetery, after which the skulls and bones are removed and the skulls artfully inscribed with the owner's name before being placed in the local *beinhaus,* or bone house, where they are something of a tourist attraction.

WILLOWLAWN HAS had its own bizarre experiences with exhumation and common graves, as I discover one morning when Scotty gets a call from a distressed housewife who explains that three or four bones of disturbingly human likeness have been deposited in her garden, adjacent to the cemetery's east fence— could they have come from Willowlawn? Having assured her that they are animal bones, nothing more, Scotty promptly dispatches Peter to pick them up and *to bury them for krisakes* before it occurs to the woman to notify the health department or the police.

"Gawdam dog bones," he says to me as he brushes past on his way upstairs for a slurp.

An hour later, as we lay out the graves for the day, Peter informs me with thinly veiled delight that the bones were indeed human, and that this is not the first time such macabre detritus has shown up on neighbourhood lawns. He says Scotty once told a woman who lived nearby that bones of any sort—birds, monkeys, dinosaurs—are carried into the area by underground streams, sometimes from as far away as China. Any human bones, on the other hand, are "remnants of ancient civilizations," perpetually pushed upward by ground pressure, a process accelerated in these days of planetary disturbance by the actions of hydro and sewer crews (but of course never by gravediggers or gardeners).

The bones, Peter informs me nonchalantly, come straight out of the Quarry, where there are "hundreds of them" in various phases of decomp and disintegration. The Quarry is a fifty-by-eighty-foot crater on the south border of the cemetery, protected from public view by a dense arc of white cedars. Until now, I have known it only as a dump for prunings and grass clippings and for the yard or so of clay and sand that is displaced every time another coffin is lowered into the ground.

Peter says that several years earlier the cemetery's owners quietly ordered the evacuation of three hundred or more "welfare graves" from the potter's fields in the oldest sections of the graveyard. These, he points out, were "city" burials, unidentified bodies—no grave stones.

"They emptied the plots," he says, "cleaned them up and resold them."

He says the same thing has happened in the cemetery's more refined sections, where a high-end plot, a "multiple," can cost as much as a Chevy Impala, and where one might expect the dead to be safe from corporate predation. The rule of thumb, he says, is "ten years without a stone or any sign of tending" and if you're a stiff, you better watch out, you might soon be looking at daylight.

The cemetery, he claims, has been monitoring such graves for half a century, cued by poorly attended, or even unattended, burials. Peter has seen people buried in two-thousand-dollar graves, in five-thousand-dollar bronze coffins, with just a single mourner in attendance—or in one notable case with no mourners at all.

I am struck more by the pathos of a burial without mourners than by the brutality of the uprooted grave, although I demand to know immediately what sort of graves, with what sort of inhabitants, end up getting ripped out of the ground? Predict-ably, it is those of men or women with no mates or relatives—"nobody to put up a stone or bring flowers." Apparently, there is a local humanitarian organization whose sole purpose is to supply "mourners" for funerals that are likely to be sparsely attended. "Just like Hollywood," says Hogjaw, where he claims casting agencies routinely hire out D-cup sympathizers and lantern-jawed pallbearers for entertainment-industry funerals—those likely to be seen on television.

The grave-raiding is said to have been mothballed a couple of years ago when a Hungarian woman showed up looking for the grave of her grandfather, who had fled Hungary and come to Canada during the mid-1950s. He had died before any other family member arrived and, family records showed, had been buried in Willowlawn. As it turned out, the grave in which the man had been planted in 1956 had been scooped a decade later, resold and, by the time the woman visited, had already been capped with a stone. Suspecting she might know the where-abouts of the grave, perhaps even have documentation, Scotty took her to the nearest unsold plot, which as fate would have it was one of the most expensive in the cemetery. His fiscal folly did not become clear until a week later when an elaborate stone arrived for the grave, which Scotty had no choice but to install and leave standing, wiping from the slate several thousand dol-lars in potential profit.

The plot, Peter says, is one of three he knows of in the cem-etery bearing headstones that do not represent the remains below. The other two, he confides, are the result of a mix-up from several years back, which occurred on a day when both he and Scotty were away and Pirmin the German led a funeral to a pre-pared grave within thirty or forty yards of where a second grave had been dug for use the same afternoon. Only when a headstone arrived for one of the plots a few weeks later did Scotty realize that Pirmin had been confused by the intricate plot maps, and that the corpses had been buried in the wrong graves. So as not to befuddle the records, Scotty allowed the stone to be placed according to the map, not the body. He told Peter that, in time, both sets of remains would be dug up and shifted, a relatively simple task given that both had been dropped into outer vaults.

"But they never were," laughs Peter. "Too much effort—plus, he has to pay me triple time to take a grave apart."

As we return from the snack truck, I ask Peter whether disturbing a grave months after a burial wouldn't provoke questions among the relatives of the dead, to which he responds with his usual patient alacrity that a disinterment, particularly an illegal one, would never be undertaken at a time when anybody was likely to witness it. He recalls a night a few years back when he was summoned to the cemetery at 2 A.M. and ordered by Scotty to dig up a grave, the remains from which were placed in a refrigerator crate and spirited from the graveyard on the back of a flatbed truck. And another night when, digging by flashlight, he and Hogjaw attracted a passing police car which he says booted it straight into the cemetery, cherry flashing, to see what was going on—and booted it straight back out when Scotty invited them over to the grave to confirm that everything was being done in compliance with the disinterment statutes. One of the cops, he says, "took a step toward the spookhole, caught a whiff, and they were outta there as quick as they'd come in."

As for telltale signs of disturbance, he and Hogjaw are capable, he says, of taking a grave apart and "putting it back together so that nobody would ever know it had been touched." Their meticulous attention extends to the vacuuming of stray flakes of soil from the surrounding sod and the "fluffing" of the grass, a kind of blow-drying process, in places where the digger tires have flattened it. Sinkers, he reminds me, get repaired every day, and no one is the wiser.

THE CITY, I would discover later in the summer, had for some time been sending as many as a hundred unclaimed corpses a year to city cemeteries—mostly at a point when they had begun to stink up the morgue. In fact, on a day in late June, I was involved in such a burial—a grotesquely unpleasant event for which the unidentified victim of a Parliament Street fire arrived not in a hearse but on the bed of a two-ton City Works truck, and not in a coffin but in a heavily taped cardboard box, the sort in which one might expect to receive a shipment of, say, carpeting or window blinds. On the top, someone had written "SMELLY LORRAINE F" and, using the same marker, had mapped out half a dozen games of X's and O's.

Scotty says the city cemeteries have for years argued against burial and in favour of cremation for what he calls "the civic stuff"—or at very least for burial in common graves, as a way of saving time and "storage capacity," a term used in the industry to refer to the seventy-odd cubic feet of space that is the real nugget of commerce once the rose gardens, shade trees and "eternal maintenance" have been factored out of the exchange.

"It's land," says Scotty. "They're not making it anymore."

Unfortunately, as he points out, "they are still making human beings" (and will be, he says, until sex gets painful). "And all of them," as he puts it, "need a place to stand up and eventually a place to lie down"—unless, as he points out, they are "roasted," cremated, which in the case of civic indigents would represent something of a gain for the cemetery business.

Willowlawn, he submits, will eventually be "so full of stinkers," including his own, there will be no place to put them and no profit left for those clever enough to have come up with the idea of wresting the planet from those who live on it and selling it back to them at an exorbitant mark-up in burial-sized portions.

"At that point," he says quite cheerfully, "the whole gawdam enterprise will be allowed to run to weeds."

If there is hope for Willowlawn as a business—which is to say hope beyond the fifty years of money-making that lie in its immediate future—such hope, Scotty speculates, exists in the building of a multi-storey mass mausoleum, a kind of condo of tombs, in which thousands of bodies will be accommodated at prices that, according to Scotty, will make even "the platinum option" in the Garden of the Apostles of the Living Christ look like a door crasher at Honest Ed's.

He further speculates that, if cremation smoulders as an option, the long-term future may be in what he calls "cemetowers"—sixty- or seventy-storey "memorial" structures, buildings with thousands of grave-sized offices, emeritus cubicles, for the planet's permanent retirees. Such structures would incorporate interior technology of a sort that would, for example, use the heat produced by decomposition to keep interior space warm in winter and use effluent methane to run air conditioning in summer. Peter tells me that if I want to see what level of heat is produced by the decomposition of the newly dead, I need only come into the cemetery in late March, when the snow is gone from the new graves as much as two or three days before it disappears off graves in which corporeal rot has given way to the cooler and more peaceable corruption of wool suits, cotton shirts and linen dresses.

More realistically, Scotty can see a time when entire municipalities will be organized around the cemetery business, well away from areas of high population. There is apparently already such a place, Colma, California—"a necrrropolis" as Scotty refers to it—built during the early century so that San Francisco cemeteries could be cleared of their inhabitants in the interest of eliminating the "diseases" that were thought to breed in crowded urban cemeteries. "The only disease ever identified," he sniffs, "was the lack of a profitable return on prime real estate." Not surprisingly, the vacant cemeteries eventually fell to developers, which, better than the dead, Scotty says, used the land for the purpose God created it—which was of course the turning of a buck.

PETER'S MOST striking contention about burial and disinterment at Willowlawn is that for years Scotty has survived intense company pressure to retire by threatening to go to the newspapers and to spill his guts about the cemetery's nefarious practices.

"Why's it so important he retire?"

"Because he's a fucked-up old drunk!"

Peter says that Scotty has not only documented Willowlawn's secrets but has placed those secrets with a lawyer, to be made public if he should happen to meet with any harm. He adds nonchalantly that Scotty is "afraid they're going to kill him."

"Afraid *who's* going to kill him?"

"Afraid *they* are," he says, conjuring for me a mysterious cabal of corporate cutthroats running their murderous empire from some windowless silo in Mississauga.

"Guys like Al?" I ask.

"Guys *including* Al," he says, a reference to Al Faragazzi, the company's saturnine business manager, who occasionally drops by in his black Buick LeSabre (in his all-black clothing and cowboy boots) and huddles with Scotty in the upstairs office.

What Peter does not tell me—it eventually reaches me in dribs and drabs—is that, by rights, he himself should be Al's first lieutenant at Willowlawn. Apparently, he was hand-picked by Al and brought to Willowlawn to be groomed as Scotty's successor and for five years has seen his career pinched by the old man's pigheaded refusal to move on. The fact goes a long way to explaining the contempt the two hold for one another and the mean-spirited politicking that is a running theme of even the most trifling of their interactions.

What Peter does tell me is that Al has several times ordered him to dump fresh fill into the Quarry in an attempt to bury its secrets. The problem, shrugs Peter, is that ground pressure and frost keep pushing the bones to the surface. "And the dogs and coons just keep digging down to get them."

Seven

DEATH'S LITTLE ACRE

THAT SAME afternoon, Scotty assigns me to perhaps the plum-
miest of cemetery jobs: cruising the recent graves, picking up
spent flowers and hauling them to the Quarry in the antique flatbed wagon. At Scotty's insistence, and to his credit, his employees, including myself, approach the chore with considerable
delicacy, grazing the flowers selectively, removing the worst
of them and consolidating what remains into a smaller, tidier
display.

One of the more unlikely offshoots of such cruising is the
practice, engaged in mainly by the year-round employees, of
gathering up a dozen or so roses or gladioli off a new grave and
taking them home, to be reinvented as a living room or dining
table bouquet. It is said of Pirmin the German that occasionally on Fridays at quitting time, he would fill the trunk of his car
with roses and carnations, clean them up when he got home and
then head downtown to sell them on Yonge Street or in York-
ville for fifty cents a stem.

Weeks earlier, intrigued by the allure of free flowers, I myself
pulled a dozen pink roses from a new grave, took them home
and handed them rather sheepishly to my mother, a lifelong

pragmatist and amateur florist, who could take even the stingiest assortment of hawkweed and sweet peas, shake it with a little bracken and set out an elegant summer bouquet. And now she quite happily dandied up *les fleurs de mort* and placed them in a vase on an end table in the living room of the family apartment.

As fate would have it, my older sister, home from university in Boston, entered the apartment a few minutes later and, without so much as a greeting, walked to the flowers, glared at them dispassionately and demanded to know where they had come from.

"They're mine," I said.

"Where did they come from?" she said quietly.

"What's wrong with them?"

"Just tell me where they came from!"

"Why?"

"Did they come from the cemetery?"

"They came from the florist's, and there's nothing wrong with them."

She took a step toward them, glowered into their negligibly soiled blossoms, then back at me, and said, "They're from that horrible cemetery, aren't they!" And with contemptuous finality she wrenched them from their vase, stomped from the living room and flung them off the sixth-floor balcony onto Park Vista Avenue.

A MORE fulfilling pleasure of such cruising lies of course in meeting the people, the dozens of pedestrians and cyclists who drift in and out of Willowlawn in the course of a summer's day. Some of them stay only as long as it takes to walk from gate to gate, others for hours, sunbathing or reading or getting stoned. Some stay a night, or several nights, particularly when "Bad Emma" is among them, running what is reputed to be a pocket-change whore service somewhere out in the Garden of the Apostles of the Living Christ.

During the mid-afternoon, as I cruise the new graves, I come upon an emaciated middle-aged man, a gaunt cartoon of humanity, sitting with his shirt off beside a weed-ridden stack of drainage pipes in a back corner of the Garden of the Blessed Redeemer. He has a savage tan that in places has puckered into sores, and the bones in his face and shoulders seem on the verge of ripping through the membrane that is his skin. As I approach, I can see tucked into the pipes an array of bags and bottles, plus the supply of aging newspapers all but intrinsic to the modern street tramp's existence. Far from growing defensive, as I had anticipated, this scabby interloper returns my greeting with the nonchalance of an old classmate. "I gather you're an employee," he says brightly and, as if to affirm his stature among the minions of the institution, informs me that he has had several chats with one of my *"campagnos,"* adding that the big Italian has accorded him an unequivocal welcome, warning him about Scotty and advising him to keep an eye peeled for the "death-green Vauxhall."

"Name's Leo," he says raising his eyebrows, bending slightly at the waist in mock gentility. His forearms are spotted with dime-sized scabs and look as if they had been chewed on by dogs. *"I know, I know!"* he says, anticipating me, "I should see a doctor! That's what everybody tells me! And I've seen one." He says his problem, diagnosed a year ago, is "just" skin cancer and that three days is the anticipated stay in hospital if he has his lesions removed surgically. So he is waiting until winter, when he can take advantage of the warmth of the ward—"and of course the nurses," he adds, hinting at some modest fetish for sponge baths, white stockings and the like.

In the course of conversation, he tells me he was for a decade a United Church clergyman in the Northwest Territories, and at times over the years has been a taxi driver, roofer, hotel chef, and security guard at the Tampax factory in Barrie. He has been, of all things, a book reviewer for *The Socialist Report.* "Book reviewing," he announces sonorously, "is the final mustering ground of lost souls and drunken theologians," of which he claims to be both.

He says in winter he spends six hours a day in a variety of city libraries, as well as seven or eight a week in the Christian Science Reading Room and at Rochdale College, where he is, he says, "the sex and drug counsellor."

However, he is considerably more guarded about the specifics of his presence at Willowlawn—is not so much "living" here, he says, as "vacationing," taking a sabbatical from his winter round of shelters, public washrooms and libraries. The shelters, he explains, are "bad enough at the best of times, but in the hot weather . . . Well," he says, "imagine forty guys who haven't had a bath in weeks taking off their pants in one room at one time, in ninety degrees of heat." The worst of it, he adds, is that most of them are sick or have lice, and he describes a stink-coded array of diseases and bodily dysfunctions that, on her strongest day, would have driven Mother Teresa from the ward. "When people tell you it's dangerous in the shelters," he confides, "what they don't tell you is that you're more likely to die of asphyxiation than of a knife in the back. Which is why I come here!" he brightens, noting the fresh air, the flowers, the meteors of August. "The other night when it rained, I slept right there in that big pipe, cozy as a teddy bear . . . Look!" he says, lurching to his feet. He reaches into a length of drainage tile and extracts a well-weathered copy of Dostoevsky's *The Brothers Karamazov.* "Found it in those couplings," he says.

I explain to him that it undoubtedly belongs to his benefactor, *il campagno,* who has created an al fresco library at Willowlawn by sequestering books in, for example, the eaves of the shit house, in the pile of concrete vaults behind the shop and in the stone foundation of the flagpole in the Garden of Eternal Remembrance.

He is several puffy thoughts into a commentary on the Russian novelists when, quite suddenly, the muscles sag discernibly around his mouth and eyes. A minute later, there is a silence and he says, "I don't mean to compromise your hospitality, my young friend, but the scripture had it wrong when it said one cannot live on bread alone. I suspect that a man in my circumstances could live quite nicely on bread alone—maybe with just a little tobacco and sherry. Quite to the contrary, it's *literature* we can't live on." He pauses to organize his thoughts, leans forward and with a gesture of his hand takes in his surroundings. "As much as I enjoy the amenities in Death's Little Acre," he says, "you can imagine I'm not here entirely by choice. Which being the case, my friend, I might inquire if you could spare me a dollar?"

Having extorted the last coins from my pocket, Leo walks to the far end of the pile of pipes, reaches into his secret pigeon-hole and withdraws a shopping bag and a crushed pack of store-bought cigarettes. Uttering prayerful volleys of gratitude, cut with grovelled apologies over his "despicable manners" in vacating the pleasure of my company, he steps out spryly in the direction of the local liquor store.

A glance into the pipe ends reveals among other things a half dozen Mennen aftershave bottles, a battered roll of toilet paper of the same exfoliating variety used in the employees' outhouse, and a quart bottle of Chinese cooking wine.

In an adjacent pipe, hidden in shadow, lies a surprise that hints at the presence of a personal deity, or perhaps a genie with a will to fulfill old wishes. I am speaking of a sheaf of staple-bound pages, poorly mimeographed, from a book entitled *Vanishing the Elephant*, a kind of "how-to" on the performance of magical tricks—a book that, from my childhood fascination with magic, I have known about for years and once craved owning but never did because of its price (I think forty dollars at a time when a paperback crime novel cost twenty-five cents). When I asked for it on my eleventh birthday, my dad told me it was for "serious magicians," inadvertently imbuing it with an allure that for me it has never shed.

And now here it is in my hands, as illicit-seeming as ever, and as enticing, in particular because its fourteenth page describes what for me as a child was the ultimate sleight of hand, "the snake trick," a preposterous deception whereby a rope is fed into a verifiably empty tube, emerging from the other end as a fat live snake. I have seen the trick performed only once, when my father, a middling amateur magician, took me in 1960 to the annual magicians' convention at Colon, Michigan, where we toured the Colon Magic Factory and attended half a dozen performances by magicians who my father believed were the most accomplished at the event. One of them was an oily Egyptian in a fiery orange turban, who for his finale cradled a length of plastic pipe in his lap, fed a yard or so of hemp rope into one end of it and coaxed from the other a live milk snake, about an inch in diameter, presented suggestively as a deadly cottonmouth or rattler. As the snake slithered lazily up the Egyptian's arm, my father leaned over and whispered to me, "It's coming out his sleeve."

"How does it get from his sleeve into the pipe?" I whispered.

"I don't know," my father said, and then after the performance, "That's why they call it a trick."

It is perhaps telling to report that what most captivated me during three days in Colon were neither the shows nor the supply shops nor the chance to meet the performers, but the magician's graveyard on the outskirts of town. Some of the headstones bore carved motifs of tricks being performed—a rabbit being pulled from a hat, a woman being sawed in two and, on the grave of a long-dead escape artist, a robust skeleton emerging, smiling, through the exploded sod of his own grave.

Sadly, the page that would have shed light on the snake trick is missing from the stapled sheaf, and having examined photos of Houdini and Blackstone at work, I slip the pages back into the pipe, grab the handle of my wagon and traipse off through Redeemer, stopping eventually at a newly plugged child's grave, where I conjure a happy eight-year-old in her party dress, bursting through the sod into the heat of the afternoon.

A week earlier, Hogjaw and I had prepared the grave, laying everything out in miniature, then had watched from a distance as the mourners arrived and a pair of young men in winter-weight suits carried a small white coffin to the graveside. In the absence of the full-sized lowering device, they set it on a pair of weathered planks that we had laid across the hole and that, conservatively speaking, would have supported a dead elephant.

"Boy or girl?" Hogjaw had asked the undertaker as we lowered the box with hand straps.

"Girl," and after a few seconds, "Did you want to see her? (It was a question posed not of disrespect but out of the functional pride with which all embalmers and morticians go about the business of preparing a body, particularly the face, for public viewing and burial.) That we might reject the opportunity to pay our respects in this final innocuous way seemed as heretical as it might have seemed to open the coffin. But as I was about to accept a peek, Hogjaw uttered an emphatic "No fucking way," then leapt onto the digger and pushed a yard or so of greyish brown clay in on top of the box.

NOW, A week later, I arrange what remains of the bouquets into a raggedy hummock of crudely edited roses and gladioli, managing in the process to salvage three or four collapsible wire frames of the sort that florists use to support their wreaths and arrangements. By the time I have cleaned up two dozen graves on the east side of the cemetery, I have collected nearly fifty such frames and have fussed them into a heap atop the rotted and stinking flowers that now nearly fill the flatbed wagon.

I head for the shop, where Scotty materializes, scoping my cargo with greater than customary avarice. He immediately orders David to unload the frames and drag them into the padlocked chamber where he keeps hundreds of them in a ramshackle tangle. Every few months, a floral supply dealer drops by, pays him fifteen cents a piece and trucks them off for refurbishing. Scotty has explained to me more than once that if ever I see anyone else so much as looking at the frames, let alone picking them up, I am to inform him immediately. It is Hogjaw's contention that given a choice between "eating shit," as he puts it, and allowing Peter or Luccio to share the income from this modest recycling scam, Scotty would tuck happily into a plate of "fresh brown" as newly dropped feces are referred to at the cemetery. And they are referred to. Every morning, the assignment board in the shop designates one of us for "brown patrol." The odious job requires David or Norman or myself—or, occasionally, Luccio or Hogjaw—to scour the back acres, particularly along the fences, scoop in hand, gathering up after the transients who sleep under the shrubs and invariably at some point in the night wander onto the lawns and reintroduce to the weather the indigestible wastes of their consumption of wieners, Wonder Bread and Aqua Velva. Such patrols were instigated because twice during the past year Scotty has received complaints from undertakers whose sorrowing clients have had their dignity vitiated by the unwelcome discovery of what is clearly human shit on the soles of their Ferragamos or Florsheims. It is bad enough that the homeless, the infidels, reside in a place intended to be the exclusionary preserve of the worm-ravaged corpses of respectable urbanites. But that they drop their turds here in Charnalville is, to Scotty's mind, tantamount to death itself, to death's trauma, particularly when measured against the delicate sensibilities of the newly bereaved.

The "feces neurosis," as Peter calls it, has reached such a state that, prior to bringing a potential investor into a given part of the cemetery, the plot salesmen routinely make a reconnaissance, a visual sweep, of the locale, ostensibly for candy wrappers and dead birds but really of course for fresh brown.

FOR REASONS unknown, the cemetery's other significant poop-seeking operation—generally referred to as "dog detail"—is conducted as if dog feces and human feces were unrelated commodities, both of which just happened to come out of the lower bowel of high-level, warm-blooded vertebrates. They are never stalked together—I suspect in part because one tends to appear in the morning, after the night drifters have been afoot, the other in the late afternoon, after the dog walkers have made their rounds.

"Dog shit in Holy Blessed Virgin—H-520," Scotty will bark at one of us as he staggers in from his afternoon rounds. "Get out there and take care of it!" And off one of us trots, scoop and bucket in hand.

One day when he is about to embark on dog detail, David asks his grandfather whether perhaps it would be an advantage to post a sign or two urging dog walkers to pick up after their animals. He claims to have seen the same fat Labrador retriever unleashed and crapping in The Garden of the Last Supper every day for a week. "Yes, yes, of course it would," whispers Scotty, "problem is it would remind everybody we have dogs here—we have dog shit here."

David is keen to put out poison, to which Scotty responds that, while it's "a lovely thought," the last time he put out poison in an attempt to rid the place of an enemy—namely the rats in the Quarry—he inadvertently knocked off a family of skunks (which over a period of days were transported in fertilizer bags by Pirmin the German to the shores of Lake Ontario, below the Bluffs, for impromptu burial at sea).

Only later does it come to light that there is already a dog buried in the cemetery, that in fact *Scotty's* dog is buried here— in fact, Scotty's *Scottie* dog is buried here (or more accurately Scotty's Scottish wife Catherine's Scottie dog)—whose beloved remains Scotty is said to have brought in the trunk of his car on a winter day, taking the animal by the hind leg and tossing it, frozen stiff, into a grave that was about to be plugged in the Garden of the Last Supper. Asked by David a day or two later if it is true that Thistle is buried in "Last Supper," Scotty claims it was David's grandmother, not he, who insisted on a decorous burial for her beloved companion of eighteen years. Feigning laughter, Scotty submits that his wife loved the dog more than she loved her own husband—a jest in which there is just enough pathos and implied pain that no one cracks a smile until Luccio suggests that perhaps the dog was a better lover than Scotty. Fortunately, it is noon hour, a point in the day by which Scotty is sufficiently oiled that the comment drifts past him, and the desultory and equivocating labours of the morning tip irreversibly into the desultory and equivocating labours of the afternoon.

eight

NO TIME TO CROAK

DURING THE third week of July, two or three days into a mumser of a heat wave, rumblings begin to surface about a city-wide gravediggers' strike. Not that it hasn't been expected. The union local has been without a contract for six months, and, strategically, the time and temperature are right. The thought of unburied corpses piling up in ninety-degree heat is about as attractive to cemetery management as it is to the city at large.

"It's no time to croak," chirps Peter, who, based on a newspaper article he has read, informs us that when the strike happens the psychological trauma will be such that the death rate itself will drop, as it apparently did during the last strike a half-dozen years ago. The next day, he pins up a *Globe and Mail* story entitled "Knowing When to Die," which describes the conclusions of a trio of Berkeley psychologists who have discovered that the dying not only have the "capacity to cling to life for indefinite periods of time," but that they will exercise that capacity for reasons as simple as their desire to "celebrate a landmark birthday" or "spend Christmas with family" or "be present at the impending visit of a loved one." Or, under present circumstances, to

avoid having their carcasses trapped, restless and rankled, above
ground during the unionized shutdown of their local cemetery.

On the day news of the strike hits the newspapers, a raffish
old man accosts Luccio and me in the Garden of the Last Supper, telling us that if he'd known we were unionized, he'd have
"bought a plot someplace where they've never heard of gawdam
unions!"

Luccio contemplates this for a second, turns to face the old
man and says in a modulated voice, "Notwithstanding that I am
not a union employee, sir, I submit to you in all due respect that
in places where they've never heard of gawdam unions—and I
speak here of advanced strongholds of human tolerance such as
gawdam China and gawdam Soviet Russia—they do not *need*
cemeteries because they dispose of their dead by grinding them
into sausage and spitting out the gawdam toenails! . . ."

Luccio pauses briefly, then delivers to the old man the glad
tidings of his good fortune: that it isn't too late for him "to buy
another plot" in any cemetery he might "gawdam choose to
go to."

"And it isn't too late for me to report you to the management!"
sputters the old man in his papery voice.

"Actually," responds Luccio, glancing at his watch, "it probably is too late, inasmuch as all complaints about the non-union
help must be submitted to the management before the management passes out from alcohol mortification at approximately
3 P.M."

THE UNION local, though small in itself, is an affiliate of the
more powerful Teamsters Union, which, during the strike of '63,
provided picketers and agitators—"thugs," in Scotty's argot—
anywhere a union presence was required. While only two of
Willowlawn's employees are union members, labour law and

the union contract prohibit any of the rest of us from conducting burials in their absence. "See," says Hogjaw one day at lunch, beckoning me toward a greasy copy of the union contract on the shed wall. He locates the pertinent clause and, in a liturgical drone, reads, *"No person shall carry out a burial in any cemetery under union contract unless a member of the Gravediggers Union or International Brotherhood of Teamsters is present upon the premises, nor without the approval...* " etc., etc.

"And what happens if we do?" I ask.

"You don't," he says.

"If we strike," grumbles Peter from behind us, "nobody around here so much as cuts a piece of sod. Even taking a coffin from a hearse is forbidden."

"What if they tell us to?" says Norman.

"They won't," says Peter. "And if they do, you refuse. And you tell us. And we take action. Your allegiance is to us, not them."

Peter notes that during the last strike, one city cemetery attempted to "scab" its burials, and within a day was shut down by picketing Teamsters. "Twenty of them," he says. "Wouldn't even allow a funeral *into* the place—sent 'em back where they came from."

Norman inquires as to what happened at Willowlawn.

"Stored 'em in the chapel," pipes Hogjaw. "Eight-day strike— eighteen stinkers when we got back. That was October. This is going to be different."

JUST HOW different we can't begin to guess until the morning after the August civic holiday, when we arrive for work and, true to rumour, discover that Peter and Hogjaw have abandoned their posts and are ambling around outside the front gates, wearing shorts and T-shirts and carrying strike placards that declare,

"THE DEAD DESERVE BETTER" and "DON'T TURN OUR CEM-
ETERIES INTO AN UNDERGROUND ECONOMY."

Hogjaw is walking a muzzled German shepherd, lending
a no-nonsense presence to the picket. Around the dog's neck
hangs a smaller placard bearing the hand-printed message:
"DOG DAYS AT THE GRAVEYARD."

AT EIGHT sharp, Scotty assembles the rest of us in the shop and
issues orders that there be "no frrraternization" with the strikers.
"And if either of them sets foot on the place, I want it reported
to me immediately." We are, he says, to consider ourselves his
"eyes and ears."

"What if they speak to us first?" demands Norman, his fingers dancing over the frets of his invisible guitar.

Scotty walks toward him, puts his hand on Norman's shoulder and says, "Do you know what frrraternization means, boy?"

"Hanging around?" guesses Norman.

"Hanging around with *them*," whispers Scotty. "I don't even
want you going near them! If they speak to you first, simply
bend over backwards, put your head up your airrrse and walk
on by—*no frrraternization!*"

Luccio asks idly about contact during off-hours.

"If you'd like to talk to them, Lewcheeo," trills Scotty, "feel
absolutely free to go out there at faive o'clock and convairrrse
until the Lord restores Babylon! Enjoy yourself! Give them
my best! But when you're in here being paid, you've got better
things to do."

We emerge from the shop in unrestrained anticipation.
School is out. A service truck pulls into the driveway carrying a
trio of industrial air conditioners—30,000 BTUS apiece. Scotty
directs the driver and his sidekick to the chapel and orders Luccio and me to give them a hand.

The chapel is a beige brick building, in effect a miniature church, with laminated wood arches and windows of piss-coloured glass. During the depths of winter, the place is used for committal services and occasionally for full funerals. But for the next little while it is to be a temporary mausoleum, a crude cold-storage facility, for the corpses of the newly deceased.

With a sense of urgency uncharacteristic at the cemetery, we remove window sections and bolt the air conditioners into place. Each is mercilessly heavy and inspires a bender of bleated profanity aimed in about equal parts at the machines before us and at the Lord Jesus Christ Almighty. And of course at Scotty "the old bastard" . . . Scotty "the old cocksucker" . . . Scotty the universal slag horse who, like gods great and small, would, if he did not exist, have to be invented for such purposes.

At about noon, the truck driver, who doubles as an air-conditioning technician, brings the first chiller to life, then the next. Within seconds the place is a howling cell of Arctic turbulence. Luccio and I evacuate pronto, only to meet Scotty trundling purposefully toward us, with Norman in tow. The four of us gaggle up and Scotty explains briskly that, unlike the last strike, corpses can no longer be stored unaccompanied in a public place. By some recently altered interpretation of the statutes, the chapel has been redefined as a public place—at least when the cemetery is open. With an enthusiasm bordering on the sadistic, Scotty informs us that, once the funerals "stairrrt coming in" one of us will have to spend work hours in the building on watch over the stiffs.

The good news is that, in the heat wave, the temperature inside is unlikely to fall below freezing. What's more, Scotty has thoughtfully ransacked the lost-and-found and has located felt-lined boots and an old military parka to be worn by whoever is named to this rarified cold-weather posting.

"Who's it going to be?" he says merrily.

"Norman," says Luccio.

"Good," says Scotty and, addressing himself to the non-plussed guitar player, he says, "Rrreport to my office at two o'clawck. We've got a fewneral in at two-thirrrty and another at three-thirrrty."

Because there will be no actual burials during the strike, committal services will be held on the lawn by the chapel. But not until everybody is gone are we to move the coffins inside. Indeed, should any unauthorized soul, even a relative, attempt to enter the deep-freeze, we are to spare no ugliness in keeping them out. "And nobody from the gawdam newspapers," says Scotty. We are urged, particularly, to keep an eye out for photographers. There isn't a photographer or newspaperman in the city, he believes, who wouldn't love to get a story on what he calls "a pile of stinking coffins."

David tells his grandfather that Peter has informed us it is against the union contract for us to move coffins or even to lift them. Scotty ponders this briefly and responds that it is not against the contract for management to move coffins, and for that reason he is temporarily promoting all of us to management positions, each of us to take charge of a section of the cemetery. Norman, for example, will manage the Garden of the Blessed Redeemer, while I will run The Garden of the Apostles of the Living Christ. Luccio is placed in charge of The Garden of the Holy Blessed Virgin.

That afternoon, the *Telegram* carries a tiny report on the strike, headlined "Grave Workers Dig In." The puns are an abomination. The strikers' demands are described as "deeper wages and benefits." A photo of Hogjaw parading solemnly in front of Willowlawn appears on page two, the message on his placard clearly visible above his head: "DIGNITY FOR THE DIGGERS ASSURES DIGNITY FOR THE DEAD."

By quitting time, the strikers are in possession of the newspaper and display the picture proudly as we leave by the front gate.

Scotty's warnings notwithstanding, I slow down to exchange a word with Peter, who scribbles his phone number on a piece of newspaper and hands it to me, insisting that I call if any attempt is made to bury the accumulating corpses.

FOR THE first three days, temperatures are moderate, but on the fourth day the heat returns out of the southwest, and by noon the temperature is a windless ninety-four degrees. There are now eight coffins in the chapel, stacked as neat as timbers in a dock crib.

While the rest of us work topless and in shorts, Norman is on duty in a toque, gloves and the wretched old parka that Scotty has salvaged from the scrap heap. Like a lonesome Sasquatch he appears occasionally at the chapel's back window, peering out through the amber glass. Four or five times a day he emerges into the heat, nose dribbling, eyes puffy, looking as if he had been shot across the Styx from some deathly parallel universe. Which in a sense he has. One of us relieves him at lunch hour and during coffee break. However, as much as possible I avoid even discussion of when it might be my turn to go more regularly into the air-conditioned morgue.

During coffee break of the fifth day, Luccio marches into the chapel as I stand watch in the communal parka. A new coffin has arrived, and he flips open the lid, having heard that the corpse is that of a notorious city musician, the victim of a car accident. But as quickly as he does so he drops it again and stands there gazing across the coffin tops, contemplating, as he puts it, "the nature of corpsedom," the bio-molecular makeup of the stiff that has come through trauma—say, a suicide or car accident. "If there *were* such a thing as a soul, Wilkins, can you imagine what this kind of experience would do to it?" He glances upwards, taps his fingernails on the coffin top.

"Wilkins," he says, baiting me gently, "maybe there's a soul, and it lasts only as long as the body."

"And then what?"

"It becomes a story," he says, and within seconds has made his return to the tropics.

TALES HAVE begun to circulate about strike violence at other cemeteries, among them a rumour that unknown Teamsters have wrecked a coffin (not to mention a funeral) by dashing the thing onto the street outside a west-end funeral parlour, dumping its occupant onto the pavement. Another alleges that strikers have inveigled a number of bereaved mobsters into a dust-up at the famous Mount Pleasant Cemetery; yet another that grave-diggers have booby-trapped Mount Pleasant with pressure-sensitive explosives to keep scab workers off the grass.

A week into the strike, Scotty tells us, with no betrayal of skepticism, that Teamsters have entered a west-end cemetery at night, have exhumed a corpse buried by scabs and have removed it from the cemetery without a trace. And that at Roselawn a dead cow has been impaled on a wrought-iron fence. (Ever on the side of the lower orders, Norman informs Scotty that he believes a human being would have made the point more impressively.) That we hear no rumours about our own sordid marble farm says more I suspect about the processes and preferences of the rumour mill than about the content of the rumours themselves.

To understand Scotty's response to it all, it helps to be reminded that he is an unapologetic consumer of the *National Enquirer* and, for a few days some years ago, is said to have beefed up his morning infusions of Cutty in response to an *Enquirer* report that aliens indistinguishable from dead human beings—in coffins no less—had inhabited North American graveyards with the intent of stealing and re-animating the residents.

The rumours of violence result in Luccio being given unexpected dispensation from freezer duty when Scotty appoints him to full-time security for the duration of the strike. His mandate is to prowl the perimeter of the cemetery, just inside the fences, watching out for intruders. Scotty, morbidly serious about the appointment, puts him through a thirty-second investiture, a sort of pep talk, and within minutes Luccio is stepping jauntily across the Garden of the Holy Blessed Virgin en route to his new responsibilities. Scotty has issued him an antique walkie-talkie that he is carrying in a leather holster on his belt. And he has a coil-bound logbook in which he is to record his movements and observations. A more important book, however, is the thick paperback copy of *Don Quixote* that he has tucked in his belt.

Ninety minutes later at coffee break, as we stand kibbitzing outside the shop, Luccio gets his first call to action, Scotty's by-now drunken burr crackling semi-intelligibly out of the little receiver, apparently describing some catastrophic development at the front gate. Less out of concern for what is happening than a fervent desire to hang on to his plum assignment, Luccio is immediately afoot. I too drift that way and discover on coming over the rise a little knot of mourners and funeral-home employees in fiery discussion with Peter and Hogjaw, who are backed at this point by a pair of lumpish Teamsters, one of whom looks as if he would love to throw a punch. At anybody. The gate is closed but not locked, and a funeral procession is strung out along the street. Fred, who is observing, has his shirt off for the first time this summer, revealing a startling knot of scar tissue where his arm once joined his shoulder. Scotty is shuffling nervously back and forth by the gate, blustering at Peter about "statutory trespass," "punitive recourse," "criminal intent and instigation."

"The only thing criminal around here," Peter hollers, "is the gawdam pay!"

"The only thing criminal around here," submits Scotty, "is the amount of work you ever did for your pay!"

Luccio steps into the tempest, swinging open the gates, demanding to know what's going on.

"Well if it ain't the sheriff!" sneers Hogjaw, affecting a gunslinger's stance.

"I want you boys to get back to ranchin now," deadpans Luccio in his best frontier drawl.

"Illegal strike action!" declares Scotty, to which Peter responds that it was Scotty himself who closed the gates on the funeral.

In Luccio's reassuring presence, Scotty waves the funeral into the cemetery, pointing the lead car toward the chapel. And when the last car is through, he reconvenes his standoff with Peter, bawling and gesticulating through the fence, the two of them deflecting one another's bitterness, absorbing just enough of it to keep their private antipathies at a constructively toxic level. But at length the urge to kill wanes, the fun is over and Scotty backs away, still firing insults, but less energetically now, until eventually he turns in retreat toward his office—or, let us say, toward his lower desk drawer, where the best possible element of this horrible day awaits him in the form of the sweet-tasting stupormaker, the fluid that launched a thousand recriminations.

Apart from this relatively harmless bit of action, the week demands of Luccio little more than uneventful walks along the fences. With hours on his hands, he steps up the pace of his writing, whipping off stories with the alacrity of Simenon, sometimes as many as two or three a day. "Listen to this," he says one lunch hour as we sit suntanning by the chainlink along the north boundary of the cemetery. He opens his logbook and reads me a hastily scrawled story about a futuristic society that has somehow managed to eradicate street crime. However, in the process it has become so thoroughly habituated to institutional and corporate crime—to graft and fraud, to political and ecological delinquency—that each year, every one of its adults is obliged to serve a number of days in prison as a sort of installment against his or her inevitable convictions.

The more personal side of the story is about an innocent young prison employee who finds himself guarding a famous politician—the minister of justice as it turns out—who is in serving his levy. As the two get to know one another, the minister persuades the young man to abandon his life as a prison guard and go into politics, where he can do something ennobling for his country, even if it does commit him to habitual duplicity and lengthy bouts in the hoosegow.

Having punctuated the story with a cackle, Luccio reads me another about an "older" man who inveigles a young woman to fall in love with him by telling her irresistibly fascinating stories—about love, about magic, about "the sweet bye and bye" as Luccio puts it. But so thorough is the old man's understanding of human limitation and the nature of love that he knows his romance will last only as long as his stories are forthcoming. He also knows that each person is sent into the world with a limited allotment of stories to tell. One night after they've made love, the knowledge that his happiness must eventually end begins to consume him, and he decides to free himself from its shadow by explaining his predicament to the young woman. However, as he tells her about the inevitable end of their happiness, he begins to fear that the very tale he is unfolding, the one about the power and limitations of stories—"about creation and dissolution," as Luccio puts it—is the last he has to offer, that his allotment is used up. Afraid to finish, he excuses himself and escapes into his study.

"If he finishes the story, it's over," shrugs Luccio. "If he doesn't, it's over."

"It's not over," I remind him, "until it's time to tell his next story, and she realizes he hasn't got one."

"A guy without a story doesn't deserve a woman," says Luccio, who, meanwhile, has stretched out on the grass and closed his eyes. I lie back a few feet away, staring off above the trees to where a sun-silvered jetliner, as tiny as a lapel pin, disappears into the west.

"When I was a kid, there was a joke," he says presently. "Why do they put a fence around a graveyard—nobody wants in, nobody wants out?" In a flash he is sitting up, then standing, brushing himself off. "And what am I these days?" he hoots. "A guard at a fucking graveyard, a human fucking graveyard fence. Imagine, Wilkins, *guarding the fucking cemetery!* I'm an absurdity!" He walks over to the fence, leans on it briefly, then picks up his logbook and stuffs it into his belt along with his copy of *Don Quixote*. He looks at me benignly and says, "Do you believe in God, Wilkins?"

I examine his face for some betrayal of irony, but it isn't there—he wants an answer.

"What do you mean by 'God'?" I ask.

"No, no, none of this butter-my-bread-on-both-sides-just-in-case bullshit. It's what *you* mean, not what I mean! Do you believe or don't you?"

"Sure," I tell him. And as we saunter across the Garden of the Apostles of the Living Christ, where I have a sinker to fix, he describes to me how when the children's writer Hans Christian Andersen was a dirt-poor kid in Denmark, he and his mother were out in a field collecting spilled grain when a bailiff appeared and ordered them to hand over everything they'd collected. "The mother refused," says Luccio, "and the guy raised a bullwhip and was about to bring it down on her when his face turned blue and he fell over dead."

Luccio flicks a hand skyward. "We're a simple race," he shrugs. "From that moment on, Andersen believed God existed—said he believed it whether God existed or not."

"Whadda you believe?" I ask, to which Luccio responds with his usual hauteur that a relationship to God should never be reduced to a belief. "When people say they believe something these days, they're talking about an opinion—*in my opinion* God exists, when what *I'm* talking about is a conviction! Is knowledge! If you're looking for God," he declares, "you've gotta know what you're looking for—to know where to look!"

"And I suppose you do."

"And I suppose you do!" he taunts, screwing up his face. "Why in Christ's name would I be standing here in five-dollar running shoes with a toy walkie-talkie on my belt if I knew where to look for gawdam God?"

He kicks a little pile of gravel, exploding it across the road, adding that if he wanted to find God—to "find *her*," as he now puts it—he'd do better looking up an earthworm's arse than he would in this "God-forsaken backwater of a cemetery."

IN SPITE of the air conditioning in the chapel, there is, after seven or eight days, a detectable odour about the place—nothing really unpleasant, just a hint in the nostrils that something is not right. By now, there are twenty-two coffins stacked up. Every air conditioner is cranked up to max cool. There is talk of installing an industrial freezer unit, but doing so, according to Scotty, would mean exorbitant costs and a reinsulation of the chapel, which could take days.

"Why don't you just send them all to a cold-storage building?" David inquires of his grandfather one morning in the shop. It isn't a bad suggestion but would be a logistical nightmare, in that it would require notarized permission from the direct relatives of every corpse involved, plus a whole new insurance program against vandalism, theft and so on. What's more, such a move would require a facility that was willing to stack a pile of human corpses in with its regular inventory of TV dinners, frozen orange juice and such.

"Besides," says Scotty, "management's attitude toward a stinking corpse is: Put a bigger clothes peg on your nose."

Because of the evolving fragrance, Norman's "hourly" breaks have become longer and more frequent—beyond which he has developed low-key bronchitis. When he is not in the chapel, he goes around hacking and snuffling into any of the revolting little rags and tissues that he keeps balled up in his various coat and pants pockets. At lunchtime of the ninth day, he complains about his condition to Scotty, who, minutes later, totters into the chapel and directly back out, declaring as he enters the shop that "anybody with any hide on his nuts" should be able to live in the chapel year-round "in no more than a net singlet . . . *You're all soft!*" he hollers as he heads upstairs for a little liquid intervention. Nevertheless, he gives Norman a half-day's transfer to grass cutting and names me as the afternoon's replacement.

The turn of events so depresses me that I can barely finish my lunch. The stink and the temperature are distressing, but I am even less sanguine about the prospect of being cooped up for half a day with twenty-two restless ghosts, each I suspect cranky to see his mortal muscle safely underground. Scotty has added an extra lock to the door because, according to David, he suspects that some demon or incubus might be drawn to the place in the night and will break in and raise hell, perhaps even initiate some necrophilic action with the stiffs. It doesn't seem to have occurred to him that an extra padlock is unlikely to hold off an incorporeal invader. Luccio tells him what he has several times told me, that according to *The Tibetan Book of the Dead,* a soul leaves a body within three days of death, so that there should be no weird animus afoot that might draw predatory invaders.

"When was it written?" Scotty asks studiously.

"In the eighth century," says Luccio, to which Scotty responds confidently that the *National Enquirer* was written just this week and, on matters that pertain to contemporary cemeteries, is obviously more insightful than "some old spook book."

At one o'clock sharp, I enter the chapel dressed in the uniform of the abominable snowman—felt boots, down parka and a pair of leather mitts whose fur lining has been reduced to a smear of filth. Scotty in his mercy has lent me a wretched old Boston Bruins toque reputed to have belonged to Pirmin the German. Having closed the door behind me, I stand shuffling my feet, peering out through the amber windows, already counting down to my first break. At one point, I am genuinely startled by a distinct creaking that seems to come directly from one of the coffins. Since childhood, I have had nightmares about the dead, and, like Scotty, am unsure what to think about the likes of the French count who busted out of his coffin at precisely the point he was being lowered into the ground (*National Enquirer*); or the Alaskan barmaid shot dead in a robbery and discovered breathing six hours later (*Reader's Digest*); or the demon-afflicted child whose coffin was found crawling with snakes (*News of the World*).

As a mid-afternoon diversion, I begin reading the fire exit instructions, which are framed under glass on the back wall. As I do so, it dawns on me that there is a second door in the chapel— a mysterious "Exit B"—a legal necessity in any public gathering place. Picking my way past the coffins, careful not to touch them, I step to the front and pull aside the faded beige drapery that covers the brick wall behind the altar. And discover a fire door! Which as quietly as possible I lever open, peering out into a jungle of unkempt shrubbery, conveniently out of view of the shop and office. Having briefly considered my options, I peel down to summer threads, step outside and settle to an hour of welcome sunshine.

At the sound of the snack truck's bell, I suit up pronto and, thirty seconds later, emerge from the chapel, collecting sidelong glances when, instead of coffee to help thaw me out, I order an icy Dr. Pepper and an Eskimo Pie.

By noon the next day, I am back in the chiller—actually in the bushes behind—this time with entertainment in the form of a stack of Scotty's antique funeral and cemetery supply catalogues. Their pages are a macabre profusion of grave trappings and mortuary accoutrements—of "lip brightener," "facial tint" and "arterial flush" . . . of rubber aprons, moulding wax and tips on the rejuvenation of "dry skin" . . . of plastic wedding rings "indistinguishable from the real thing," and "cavity replacement fluids" guaranteed to "firm without shrinkage or expansion."

A saddle-stitched pocket book published in 1922 instructs morticians in the burial preparation of what it calls "corpses whose deaths are the result of accident or mischance"—by fire, water, electrical shock. "If at all possible," advises the introduction, "the wise undertaker will prevent even the closest of relatives or friends from viewing the degraded remains of the victims of strychnine or cyanide poisoning" . . . or of hanging or the (newly invented) electric chair. One particularly ferocious chapter describes the "treatment of accident victims"—hair replacement; the attachment of rubber ears; the application of "wound filler," a fast-drying paste, the description of which bears an uncanny similarity to that of LePage's ShrinkNot autobody compound. "Deep wounds to the skull," advises the text, "should, where possible, be closed first with brass wire" and "Under no circumstances should a severed head be placed on a corpse without secure stapling and adequate camouflage for viewing."

There is occasional debate at Willowlawn over what sort of deaths create the worst, the scariest, corpses, the consensus seeming to be that drowning and fire victims trump even the victims of car accidents. "Bobbers look like frogs, crispers like toads," explains Peter, who shares a view with all others at the cemetery that it is in fact children's corpses that are the worst to deal with, the most difficult emotionally, whatever their state of wholeness or decomposition. Even Scotty, with his relative imperviousness to the horrors of the death industry, is often officially "gone for the afternoon" when a child's funeral is expected, leaving the chore of leading the procession to Peter, who in turn has been known to pass the responsibility along to Hogjaw.

Of them all, it is Hogjaw who is most unsettled by the presence of children's corpses, perhaps because it is he who has the youngest sons and daughters. It is said that he once heard a voice emanating from a child's coffin and that he has seen the souls of children drifting above their graves. ("Pink and green," he told me when I inquired, explaining that on a fall morning several years ago, in the Garden of the Holy Blessed Virgin, he had seen what he called "a mini-version of the Northern Lights," and when he investigated found beneath the fading illumination the grave of nine-year-old twins buried in 1918 during the Spanish Flu epidemic.) Even Peter, the pragmatist, tells me he feels what he calls "strange currents" around the unplugged graves of children.

One of the more literate of Scotty's texts contains a brief history of the preservation of human remains, a sub-chapter of which is devoted to "the most successful preservation ever," that of V.I. Lenin, whose remains have been on display in Red Square in Moscow since his death in 1924. According to the book, a "scientific institute" was formed during the days following Lenin's death, its sole purpose being to take care of the great thinker's carcass, which twice a week since has been "stripped of clothing, including underwear, and minutely dusted and revivified."

"That's what you call maid service!" says Peter when I mention it to him.

Scotty loves such literature and lore—was most intrigued one day when I told him about Dawson City, which I visited as a teenager, and where during winters after the Gold Rush people died by the hundreds of illnesses such as meningitis, diphtheria and scarlet fever. Given the digging tools available, it was impossible to bury them after the beginning of November, when the ground froze solid. The result was that dozens of graves were dug generically during the early fall, so that they would be available for their occupants as they were needed throughout the winter. In a book that I would read years later, author Laura Berton describes seeing such graves as a child and wondering who among her friends or family—or if perhaps she herself—might be lowered into one of them before the winter was over.

THERE IS at this moment a child's body in the chapel, brought in on the sixth day of the strike and placed in the corner, separated from the others as if to avoid contamination. Norman tells me that a few hours after the small white coffin arrived, the child's mother and father returned to the cemetery in a funeral-home limo and for an hour sat motionless on the park bench outside, then sat for another hour in the limo before rolling up the road and out the gate.

A narrow plastic security band has been placed around each of the coffins. However, as I prepare to leave late that afternoon, I am disturbed to discover that the band on the child's coffin has been shifted. Someone has had it open. What disturbs me even more is my own curiosity, my discomforting inclination to have a look.

nine

THE PACE OF MICROBES

AND WORMS

BY THE time forty frosty coffins have accumulated in the chapel, the smell has begun to seep from the place like poison. Enter Marvis, a waspish young undertaker who works for his uncle's Danforth Avenue funeral parlour and who one day at noon, having delivered the forty-first coffin and chaperoned the mourners through a brief committal service on the lawn, saunters over to where Scotty is giving us the lowdown on the afternoon and begins to berate us over the stench. "It's a gawdam disgrace bringing a funeral into this," he chides, unfurling his arm in the direction of the chapel. "Are you aware that you're the only yard in the city that hasn't been able to control its own body odour?"

"Are you aware," bristles Scotty, "that you're the only idiot hearse jockey that hasn't been able to control his gawdam tongue?"

"The least you could do is burn some incense!" scolds Marvis.

"You go get us some!" says Scotty.

Marvis, who on this particular day is driving the company hearse, as well as directing the funeral, minces off toward his vehicle and, without a glance back, lays fifty feet of premium Bridgestone up the cemetery's main road. He is well known around the cemetery, partly for his ambiguous sexuality, partly for his high-strung humour and outrageous observations on life as a madcap mortician. He is also a pretty much inexhaustible font of stories—on the corpse that kept inflating and deflating as viewers traipsed past it in the viewing salon; on the drowned woman who was brought into the funeral home wearing fifty engorged bloodsuckers; on the corpse that disappeared from the funeral home, naked, and turned up on a TTC streetcar. During my earliest days at the cemetery, Marvis told me that a year earlier he had opened the autopsy sutures on a body he was preparing and found the abdominal cavity crowded with two-ounce bags of cocaine. "I never told a soul," he said. "Just poked the sutures back in, put a shirt on the stiff, put the stiff in a box and watched that box until it went in the ground." The compelling denouement to all this is that somewhere in Mount Pleasant Cemetery, Marvis claims, lies a hundred thousand dollars worth of drugs.

More recently, he told me about an Edmonton couple who had home-embalmed an elderly aunt using laboratory formaldehyde and Absolut vodka and then had "put her to bed for a couple of years" so that they could continue to cash her pension cheques. He said he intended to write to Absolut to suggest an ad campaign, the central image of which would be a coffin-shaped Absolut bottle, the "preferred liquor" of the amateur undertaker. "And the professional, too," it occurred to him to add, knowing that morticians as much as coroners or gravediggers are party to the antique allegiance that unites the dead, the death industry and the twenty-six-ounce suckling kit that the average embalmer consumes pretty much daily with the zeal of a baby on the tit. According to Marvis, his Uncle Max inhales a bottle of Glenlivet during every embalming, straight out of the bottleneck—this compared to his grandfather who, he claims, drank half a dozen bottles of stout.

On those occasions when his own presence is required at an embalming, Marvis prepares by drinking a shot or two of his uncle's Glenlivet and smoking what he calls "a wobble stick—a fat one," and then another before dressing the corpse, a minor mortuarial art that has become something of a specialty for him over the past couple of years. "You dress 'em up right, nobody notices," he says. "You get it wrong, the poor fucker might as well have dressed himself." Marvis has seen fire victims "fried in their own fat"; has sewn the head onto a decapitated accident victim, securing it with duct tape; has more than once discovered mice chewing on the wax-enhanced lips of corpses that have been made up and laid out for burial. His worst chore as a beginner, he told me one day, was "greeting" the new corpses and "cleaning them up," which included everything from peeling off their death-saturated clothes to removing "shit and dried blood," to placing forty-pound bags of lead pellets on their thighs or knees or shoulders, so as to flatten them out before soaping and hosing them and passing them along to the undertaker. Nowadays, he allows, his first responsibility on arriving for work each morning is to "make sure there's no mouse shit on the stiffs, and no chewed spots."

But Marvis is a serious man, too. Like all of the industry's career practitioners, he possesses detailed knowledge of the pace at which microbes and worms consume first the eyes, then the genitalia, the liver and so on, until a human corpse has been reduced to spareribs. He maintains that, with modern synthetic fabrics (for the most part non-biodegradable), a stiff is likely to remain "fashionably dressed" long after its flesh and eyeballs have nourished their last sightless worm or blade of grass.

HALFWAY THROUGH lunch hour, to our surprise, Marvis wheels back into the cemetery with a box of small brown incense cones. "Here!" he says, tossing them toward Luccio who is flaked out on the grass. Marvis and Luccio share an occasional reefer, as well as ongoing banter over any number of tactless concerns, including Marvis's presumed sexual preferences. But on this occasion Luccio is clearly unequal to the repartee and, half asleep and irritable, ends any possible fireworks with a quiet "Fuck off."

Marvis beetles over to the chapel and a minute later reappears, trailing a goofball of jasmine-perfumed smoke. "If you need anything else sweetened up, let me know," he simpers as he trips past us. "Where shall I send the invoice?" he shouts at Scotty, who answers that for now he should just bring it with him the next time he needs directions to a plot site or half an hour of Scotty's time to help him with the logistics of a burial. "You're the worst gawdam undertaker in the world!" Scotty yells at him. "Your uncle must be ashamed of you!"

From the road, Marvis flashes him the finger and, bouncing into the driver's seat, paints another eighty feet of tire rubber up the cemetery's central roadway.

TOWARD THE end of its second week, with no apparent movement toward a settlement, the strike begins to lose momentum. Each morning Peter and Hogjaw show up a few minutes later for picket duty, and each afternoon they leave a few minutes earlier. From time to time, three or four horse-bellied Teamsters appear on the line, trundle back and forth in front of the gates, and disappear into the heat.

One afternoon as I tend the outer gardens with Fred, Hogjaw sidles up to the wrought-iron fence and confides that the union has been slow producing strike pay and that for a week or more he and his family have been living on vegetables from his garden. The only trips to the supermarket are for what little they can afford in the way of bread and milk. Coincidentally, the agency that distributes beer in the province is also on strike (its action timed as meticulously to the heat as is the action of the grave-diggers). However, because my sister works at Diana Sweets restaurant and has access to their dwindling supply of foreign beer, I'm occasionally able to score a couple of bottles of Tuborg or Lowenbrau—as I do that night, delivering a cold bottle to Hog-jaw the following morning in order to cheer him up.

On the strike's tenth day, perhaps on a tip from Luccio, Scotty catches Norman sunbathing in the bushes outside the chapel, relieves him of his security duties and, against my mut-tered protests, names me his replacement. At noon hour, while he is tending to Catherine, I fortify myself by sneaking into his office to gather a fresh stack of embalming and cemetery supply catalogues. Given the warped intimacy of their illustrations and product descriptions, they comprise an all but fetishistic history of the burial business.

The glacial pace of the afternoon is quickened only by my self-imposed curriculum in the antique appurtenances of the embalming industry—the clamps and cruets and rubber bot-tles—and by the arrival of the snack truck at 2:45, which brings me a brief reprieve from the crypt.

Back in the chiller, I embark on a no-nonsense essay on the modern autopsy, discovering with spellbound revulsion that practitioners of the Virchow Method begin by putting a "large Y-shaped incision" in the trunk of the corpse, folding the chest skin (plus the breasts of female corpses) back over the face while the bones of the body cavity are sawed up and "yanked" so that the "abdominal basket" can be gutted and explored.

Seeking a few seconds of escape from the heat, Luccio pops in before closing time and bangs around briefly among the coffins.

"Wanta hear something weird?" I ask, and, with his eager assent, proceed to inform him that among the bodies surrounding us, most that have been autopsied have come minus their inner organs and brains (his response to which, typically, is that even those who come into Willowlawn *alive* come, for the most part, minus their guts and brains).

I pass him the essay, which explains matter-of-factly that unless relatives request that the organs be returned to the body, they are routinely incinerated in the morgue, and that the torso, if not the skull, is bulked in with cavity filler.

Luccio pours himself into the journal, causing me brief phantom pain as he reads with gusto of how the examination of the testicles is conducted by jerking the "skinless orbs firmly up into the body cavity," where they are cut from their yo-yo strings and are scalpelled into slices.

THE FOLLOWING morning, while Scotty is with the plot salesmen, I unearth from his office a Depression-era history of the city's cemeteries. It includes a chapter on our own illustrious bone dump, which, according to Airdrie J. Honeycliffe, Ph.D., was founded in 1888 by a local order of Augustinian priests and, until 1914, was called St. Augustine's Burial Grounds. Some fifty of the original monks are in fact interred in the oldest part of the cemetery, an oval of graves that we call "The Acre," over which Scotty keeps a sporadic drunken watch, because of the delicacy of the nineteenth-century marble. At the time the book was written, during the 1930s, as many as fifty men were said to be working at Willowlawn on a federal make-work project—landscaping, laying sod, planting trees, making roads, all for fifteen cents an hour and the right to grow potatoes and raise chickens on a part of the grounds unaltered since the cemetery's days as a tobacco farm, then a sheep farm, during the nineteenth century.

The history of a cemetery is, perforce, rather leisurely of pace. However, on the third page of the chapter, I am brought bristling to attention by the comment that Willowlawn is "the only cemetery in the history of the city" in which a buried corpse is known to have been dug up and stolen outright, coffin and all, a few days after its burial in June of 1931. Any reportage of the incident is said to have been suppressed "in order to prevent public panic or outrage." It was not until the end of a two-year investigation "that the corpse of the pseudonymous Harold Halliwell, now missing, was revealed to have been that of a Hamilton-area mobster named Tony 'Lunchbucket' Cosentino."

"It's a lotta bullshit!" cries Scotty when I ask him about it. "I was here! I know!"

Cosentino, he declares, was a police informer, whom a gangster named Eddie Caruso wanted to kill. The police, he says, tried to throw Caruso off by burying an empty coffin and leaking that it was Cosentino's.

As Scotty tells it, what the police hadn't counted on was the mobster's determination to confirm the identity of the body. "They were gonna dig him up!" he hoots. "The police got wind of it and came and dug up the coffin themselves. Nobody except the cops and me ever knew the coffin was empty. Don't believe everything you read," he says over his shoulder as he turns to the stairs.

"Where is it?" it occurs to me to ask.

"Blessed Redeemer."

"Is there somebody in it?"

"Ahhhh," he says, stopping in the stairwell, his need for alcohol temporarily supplanted by his need to broker intrigue. He proceeds to explain that on a day in maybe 1948 he noticed a fresh grave in a corner of Redeemer where he knew there had not been a burial. "I look up the ownership," he says, "and if it isn't the gawdam city police department! They still own the plot!"

Scotty claims to have phoned the police, and a day later to have had a visit from a pair of detectives, who told him if he knew what was good for him he'd shut up and leave the grave alone. "And that's what I did!"

"And what's down there now?"

"Like every other grave," he chirps, "a few mildewed bones and a lotta healthy microbes." He submits that for all he knows or cares, there may be nothing down there at all.

I ask if he's ever thought of looking.

"We don't open graves," he says, staring at me as if at a suddenly untrustworthy retainer. He teeters slightly and rocks onto his toes. "Did somebody tell you we did?"

"Not at all."

"Did the Dutchman tell you that?"

"Tell me what?"

"That we open graves."

I am insistent that nobody told me anything, beginning to suspect that he can see me for the liar I am.

"That's why I've never told the Dutchman what I just told you," he says. "If he knew there was a grave out there that the cops had dug and plugged, for all I know he'd'a shovelled the damn thing up."

He extracts a promise that I will never tell Peter about the grave or about our discussion. "If he finds out," he says, "I'll know it's you who told him." And in his halting, bowlegged gait, he shambles up the stairs to ease himself out of the nasty little bout of sobriety that has thus far put too great a claim on the fading afternoon.

A week passes before I have the opportunity to ask Peter if indeed he knows anything about a plot owned by the police, and if so whether he knows who or what is in it.

He says, "If you wanta know that, you'll have to ask Scotty." He contends there was once a stone on the grave but that the cops took it off. "Some day when the old man's not around," he says, "we'll take a little soil out of it and see what's down there."

ten

A LONER AND A
ROSE GARDENER

LIKE FISH merchants, undertakers vote with their noses, and by the middle of the strike's third week, the city's morticians are exerting every possible pressure on the cemetery owners to get the impasse settled. They have modest influence over the owners, in that they are the first line of contact with the relatives of the dead and are often called upon to recommend a burial site.

The wheels of negotiation begin to grind, and on Sunday afternoon of the third week, a union call brings every gravedigger in the city to the downtown Teamsters' hall, where the men are to vote on what is being touted as "the absolute last" of the cemeteries' several wage offers.

Late the next morning, in a misty rain, a deep blue sedan arrives at Willowlawn's front gate. Peter and Hogjaw converge on the driver's-side window, protected from the drizzle by garbage-bag tunics and chunks of corrugated cardboard.

Minutes later, they walk abreast through the front gate, and the three-week strike is over.

The two of them, eighty cents an hour richer, go directly

to the change shed and pull on their work clothes, which have been hanging undisturbed where they were left. With fifty-three corpses in the chapel, there is little doubt about what needs doing.

As Scotty watches silently from the stairs in front of his office (not entirely pleased that the dysfunctional chaos of the past three weeks has come to an end), Peter mounts the digger and blows half a pound of carbon from its cylinders and pipes. Leaving it idling, he goes back inside and approaches Scotty for the plot locations. In one another's company they are as inflexible as railway spikes—and approximately as communicative. Hogjaw, whom I have been assigned to help, starts the tractor and hitches up a flatbed wagon.

The oldest corpses, some of them buried under half a dozen subsequent arrivals, must be dealt with first, which precipitates an orgy of shunting and bellyaching. Five of us go at it at once, the flurry of activity releasing trace odours both of embalming chemicals and of decomposing flesh.

With the first six coffins loaded onto the flatbed and with a more persistent rain beginning to fall, the morbid marathon of disposing of the dead begins.

By noon hour, the only employee not engaged in the process is Fred—and not because he lacks an arm. He has spent the early hours of the day removing sod from the burial plots. However, when he comes in for coffee, his face is such a distressing shade of green that even Scotty is able to see there isn't a day's work in him, and urges him home to bed.

Fred, barely able to stand up, insists on finishing the graves he has started, then at five minutes to noon climbs on his bicycle and wobbles out the main gate.

THE FOLLOWING day, our off-colour compatriot does not show up for work. Or the next day either. However, we are all too busy to pay much attention, and it is not until the following afternoon, when the fifty-third body is in the ground, that Scotty decides to look into his absence. Since Fred has no telephone, someone must be sent to check on him. If it were anyone but Fred, it is doubtful the old man would bother. But Fred has worked for Scotty for twenty-five years, and although the two of them exchange barely ten words a week they are bound by a multitude of nameless allegiances—and of course by Fred's extraordinary skills, without which the cemetery gardens would be chaos.

Since everyone else is otherwise engaged or irreversibly in Scotty's doghouse, Scotty chooses me as his emissary to the one-armed absentee. I am to take my own car and to spend no more time than is absolutely necessary to get over to Fred's, check up on him and report back. Clearly, Scotty sees the assignment as a plum—a bonus perhaps bestowed because I have remained more or less loyal throughout the strike. Yet as I drive through the east end of the city, I am struck by a foreboding that deepens as I catch my first glimpse of Fred's house, a tiny frame cottage, little more than a shack, unpainted in years and overgrown with every imaginable species of bramble and shrub. On the lawn, two wildly unkempt crabapple trees have insinuated themselves up under the eaves to the point where, in places, they have knocked off the roofing. One front window is covered in cardboard, and a rotted wooden fence is missing easily as many pickets as remain.

I tiptoe across a porch that is dangerously decayed and tap on the front door, but get no answer, so step around back, picking my way through a knee-deep tangle of cucumbers, tomato vines and unstaked beans.

The windowless back door is roughly constructed of hand-sawn boards, and getting no answer here either, I test the latch and find it unlocked.

"Fred!" I call as I ease the door open. "Are you in here, Fred?"

I step back, take a deep breath and push through the fetid air that is seeping out past me. In the dim light, a cat watches—my intrusion not so disturbing to it that it can prevent itself from meowing quietly and brushing against my leg. As I cross its kitchen lair, it leaps onto a sideboard cluttered with cans and dirty dishes and then onto a cupboard top from where it peers down, neck craned, eyes as big as pennies.

Repelled by the filth and smells, and tempted simply to leave, I step gingerly toward a front room, at whose entrance I stop, utter an involuntary yelp and step back. There, on a soiled cot beneath the window, lies Fred, motionless and seeping sweat. My first thought is that he is dead. But as I peer in at him in the shadows, I can hear his rattled breathing coming in engine-like blasts and, as my eyes adjust, can see the seismic heaving of his chest.

Unable to rouse him, I leave the house and, feeling somewhat lightheaded, approach the brick bungalow next door. A woman there allows me to use the phone to call Scotty, who greets my report with several seconds of maundering then a decisive command that I should call an ambulance.

Having done so, I reenter the house and stand waiting in the living room, eventually summoning the nerve to wipe Fred's face with a threadbare hand towel from the horrible little bathroom off the kitchen.

Desperate for light but unable to locate a switch, I open the front door, then a set of curtains, allowing a diffuse painterly wash onto the room's stacks of Polish newspapers, empty cardboard boxes, food wrappers, dirty clothes, bicycle parts, car parts, kindling for the wood stove, empty saucers that at one time held food for the cat. The dust on the shelves and windowsills is as thick as fur, the air dense with the smell of cat waste.

As I am about to retreat back outside, my attention is diverted by a gallery-framed photograph hanging in the tiny front entranceway. The frame and covering glass are blanketed in grime but not so thickly as to obscure the image of a family: a young woman, three well-dressed children and a natty young man in a double-breasted suit, all of them smiling into the camera. In the background, a tiny foreign car of some obscure Depression vintage is visible alongside a row of poplars. The brim of the young man's fedora slants rakishly across his face; his hands rest on the shoulders of his children. In the few seconds it takes me to absorb and comprehend the photograph, my impression of Fred is permanently altered. Whatever has become of the young woman or the three fine-featured children is for now a mystery, but the well-dressed man in the photograph is unmistakably Fred, one-time father, family man—now, incongruously, one-armed loner and rose gardener, forever disconnected from his past.

WITHIN MINUTES, an ambulance wheels up to the front gate and two youthful attendants, each sporting a Fu Manchu moustache, step carefully across the front verandah. *"Christ!"* one of them says as he enters the living room and gets a whiff. "Are you a relative?"

"I work with him."

The older of the two takes Fred's pulse and blood pressure and sends his co-worker back to the ambulance for oxygen and a black leather case that they rapidly unpack. Within seconds, Fred has a plastic bag of clear fluid hanging above him and an intravenous needle in the crook of his elbow. The pair withdraw together, reappearing momentarily with a substantial wheeled stretcher.

The question of medical insurance arises. Might there be a card? A number? One of the attendants asks if I'd mind having a look. "Try to hustle it," he says.

The bedroom is darker even than the living room, but on a

low stand beside a military-style cot lies a grubby canvas wallet that I recall having seen in Fred's possession. Amid a tattered array of wallet-sized Polish documents and more family photos, there is, indeed, an Ontario Hospital Insurance card, which I extract and pass to the attendant, at the same time inquiring whether he has any idea what's wrong.

"He's dehydrated, and his blood pressure's about half what it should be. Beyond that, I wouldn't wanta venture a guess."

As they carry Fred down the sidewalk, beneath the boughs of the crabapple trees, he rouses himself momentarily and opens his eyes, the whites of which are the colour of egg yolk. He stares up at his benefactors, murmurs something in Polish and lapses back into unconsciousness.

The stretcher-bearers roll him into the back of the ambulance, close the doors with a *thunk* and take off up the street. By this time, a couple of neighbours have poked their heads out their front doors.

With the ambulance gone, a lull descends on the street and on the hour. The starlings twitter on the lawns, the sun burns through the trees. If a question hangs in the weltering afternoon, with its fractured hint of consequence, it is: *What the fuck? What the gawdam hell?*

Fortunately, like the rest of humanity, I am too preoccupied to be hung up for long on any contemplation of what it means to be human or alive, or *inhuman* and alive . . . or not alive at all. For one thing I have responsibilities: must start my car, must turn on the radio, must return to work, must stop at the corner, must go go go.

As I sit briefly in my car by the curb, the distant burst of a siren knifes across the rooftops and trees. I crank the radio over to 1050 CHUM, from where the Righteous Brothers' hair-raising lament, "Unchained Melody," soars into the elm tops.

AS I enter the shop, Scotty appears at the door of his office, his fedora pulled low on his forehead. But his glare this time is not one of reproach. For once, there is something inquisitive, even fearful, in his boozy and baggy-eyed squint. He descends the stairs and shuffles to within feet of me. "Where is he?" he demands.

"On his way to the hospital."

"What'd they say?"

"They didn't know."

"Did you talk to him?'

"He was unconscious."

"What's your guess?"

"I have no idea."

"Did he look poorly?"

"He looked terrible!"

The run of revelations pitches Scotty into a stupor of sorts, and in the silence that ensues it occurs to me to inquire whether he has ever been to Fred's.

"Never," he says, and, squaring his shoulders in such a way that he appears to be in pain, he announces with regimental gravity that we have had a visit from the coroner. "We have to pull a stinker," he says.

"Pardon me?"

"Pull a stiff."

"I don't understand."

"Dig up a grave."

"What for?" I demand.

"They didn't tell me. They're coming in the morning . . . What hospital?" he calls over his shoulder as he wobbles across the shop.

"The East General," I tell him and ask if he knows whether Fred ever had any family. Without bothering to turn, and as if responding to an imbecile, he says, "I imagine he had a mother and father like everybody else."

"I mean a wife and kids."

He says, "Not since I've known him," and it dawns on me that, on the information gleaned from one visit to Fred's house, I know as much or more about him than does the man who has employed him for nearly three decades.

eleven

THE REMAINS OF THE DAY

AT ABOUT eleven the next morning, the city coroner—a florid-faced squirt with wooden posture and a Reichstag haircut—rolls into the cemetery in his silver-grey Mercedes and proceeds to lay down plans for the sickly activities that will consume the afternoon.

Peter disappears at lunch, eventually returning with copies of all three of the city's daily newspapers. He keeps the *Star* for himself, gives Hogjaw the *Telegram* and throws the *Globe and Mail* on the workbench. On the front page of each is the latest on a sensational murder trial that is gobbling up a hundred column-inches a day of the city's preferred fishwrap. For unalloyed gaucherie, the headlines are neck-and-neck with those of Scotty's beloved tabloids:

CROWN CONTENDS TUB DEATH WAS HOMICIDE

WAS RADIO ELECTROCUTION ACCIDENT OR MURDER?

CROWN ASKS THAT BODY BE EXHUMED

By way of explanation, a thirty-eight-year-old man, Albert "Sprocket" Bowness, is being tried for the murder of his ex-wife,

"Gus," who a year ago was found in the bathtub of her Scarborough apartment, apparently electrocuted by a plug-in radio that had fallen into the tub while she was bathing. Murder charges were not laid at the time, largely because the door to the apartment had been bolted from the inside, indicating that no one had come into the place or left it. However, the Crown now contends that Sprocket was indeed there, and either pushed the radio into the tub or drowned his ex-wife and then dumped in the radio to mislead police. Or that he *attempted* to electrocute her with the radio, failed, and so drowned her . . . and then slipped out over the balcony, leaving the chain on the apartment door.

Sprocket, whose clothing for the trial is reported to include a "studded leather jacket," a "hoop earring" and "motorcycle boots"—shrewdly chosen effects, observes Luccio, certain to camouflage him as just another law-abiding suburb-dweller— is said by the *Star* to have "wept openly" while relating to the court how he had warned Gus about the danger of placing electrical appliances on the tub.

The trial (to quote the political pundits) "has sparked heated debate" among my co-workers. Was it murder? Suicide? An accident?

"Why would anybody with half a whack try to electrocute somebody with a radio?" demands Peter. "He's a biker fer krisakes! If he wanted her dead, he'd'a snapped her neck. Or taken her out and capped her."

For today, at least, our interest in the case is rather sharply focused on Gus's unmarked grave within yards of the outermost fence of the Garden of the Holy Blessed Angels, one of the plainest and cheapest sections of the cemetery. Peter recalls that the young woman's burial nearly a year ago was a disorderly affair at which her relatives attempted a modicum of Christian dignity while, within yards of the gravesite, the young woman's biker pals danced to old Jerry Lee Lewis tunes, eventually circling the grave and, in biker tradition, pouring beer over the coffin as it was lowered into place.

Peter is restless about the specifics of attempting to exhume the remains from a part of the cemetery where, after a day of heavy rain, the water table has undoubtedly risen to within a few feet of the surface. "It's gonna stink like fucking hell," he says to no one in particular. He is equally disturbed over a vague recollection that Gus's coffin was "a cracker box," a low-priced casket constructed of little more than cardboard on a wood frame, the whole thing covered in grey brocade or felt. While I have never seen such a coffin exhumed (I have never seen any coffin exhumed), I am led to understand that this particular model exhibits approximately the integrity of wet pastry when disturbed underground, and that most likely coffin and contents will have to be lifted from the grave by hand—"lifted by yours gawdam truly," mutters Peter, who because of his seniority and union status will serve as point man on this ghastly *pièce de résistance* among cemetery exercises.

If there is a positive element to any of it, it's that the new union contract calls for a quadruple pay rate, through a minimum of six hours, on any disinterment work (non-union workers included). Each man involved, therefore, will collect at least three days' pay for whatever effort he puts in. For Scotty, this is no problem, as he passes the cost directly along to the provincial coroner's office, which passes it to the judiciary, which passes it to the treasury . . . which, as all government bureaucracies eventually must, passes it solemnly along to the taxpayers, who must manufacture the green stuff out of the black stuff at the core of their collective resentment.

Just after lunch, a big grey station wagon arrives—an overbuilt, overpolished roadboat, with tires as wide as basketballs, carrying three overweight men, two of them dressed in casual green hospital uniforms. Scotty slides into the front seat with the driver and directs him to the Garden of the Holy Blessed Angels where they park on the grass within metres of the grave. The coroner pulls up in his Mercedes, leading a plain beige Econo-line van whose front door is discreetly lettered with the words Ontario Provincial Police Forensics Unit.

A couple of feckless-looking lab rats step out and eye the site. Scotty has made good use of his lunch hour and is oiled to the point where he is behaving more like the *padrone* at some fes-tive company picnic than a stage manager for the grisly drama at hand. He shakes hands with everyone (excluding his own under-lings, of course), dispensing comments and compliments on everything from the spiffiness of their vehicles and work clothes to the quality of the afternoon's weather.

Peter and Hogjaw have been named to do the digging and dirty work. Luccio and I will stand by as spear carriers. Peter arrives on the backhoe, Hogjaw, as always, on the tractor, pull-ing a wagonload of shovels and implements, including Scotty's venerable water pump and, on this day, a thirty-ounce spray bomb of BalsamBlast Ultra to eliminate what its manufacturer describes as "the distressing odors that inevitably accompany death-site and grave disturbance." Scotty teeters over, pulls out his handkerchief and proceeds to whisk off any bits of dust or grime that have accumulated on the pump since his loving gaze last fell upon the thing.

As it turns out, the pump isn't needed—not even a cupful of water has accumulated by the time Peter has burrowed to a depth of four feet. At an appropriate point, perhaps six inches above target, Peter abandons the backhoe, and Hogjaw contin-ues with a hand shovel. The entire hole has been dug perhaps a foot wider than the original grave, to permit Peter and Hogjaw to burrow along both sides of the coffin, so that lifting straps can be fitted underneath. But as the coffin is exposed, Peter's earlier trepidations are confirmed; the thing is nothing but mush and will be impossible to hoist as a piece.

This precipitates a solemn private conference between Scotty and Peter, who are eventually joined by the coroner and forensics officials. They chatter inaudibly for a minute, migrate over to the grave for another look and then resume their conclave. In much the way a salient phrase will occasionally coalesce out of short-wave radio static, Peter's voice rises momentarily above the others, and the words "a helluva lot more money" sail free.

What is left of the coffin will have to be opened *in situ* and the remains brought to the surface by hand. Peter's contention is that, if he is going to perform this dire chore (as senior grave-digger, he has "first rights" under the union agreement to accept or refuse it), he wants twice the quadruple pay rate that he is already earning. The coroner is happy enough to see him paid, but Scotty cannot abide an agenda that will see his archrival and nemesis, the weasel who would have his job, drawing eight-fold wages—more than a week's pay for at most two hours' effort.

In the meantime, Luccio has struck up a conversation with one of the forensics technicians. Exactly what is it they're looking for? he wants to know. And the answer is, "Anything we can find that might refute the going testimony—or confirm it."

"Like what?" persists Luccio.

"Anything!" shrugs the technician. "Lung tissue, bone chips, skin samples. Electrocution burns the skin. The amazing thing to me," he says, "is that none of this was looked at when she died."

We are led to believe that even if the procedure turns up nothing, it will be useful to the Crown as a means of duping the defendant into thinking there is better evidence against him than there is.

Scotty and Peter, who have broken away from the group and have been discussing their differences more or less civilly, erupt now into hostilities, Scotty howling that if Peter is too selfish to accept his responsibilities on behalf of Willowlawn, he'll get Hogjaw or Luccio to do the job.

"The hell you will," says Peter. "The job's mine to take or leave. And I take it—but at fair pay."

Scotty thrusts his chin to within a foot of Peter's, rattles his teeth and makes his "last and final" offer of six times scale.

"Coffee time," snaps Peter, stomping away, then spinning to remind Scotty that the union agreement calls for "negotiated pay" on "emergency or extraordinary" assignments. "And if you don't think this is extraordinary," he says—but before he can complete the thought, the frustrated coroner steps forward and begins to dress Scotty down for wasting everybody's time. "Come on, now!" he winces. "Sort it out, and let's get on with it."

Chastened, and reminded of the larger issue, Scotty accedes quickly, and in no time Peter and Hogjaw are easing themselves into pale green rubberized suits and fitting gas masks to their deeply tanned faces. From the rear of the station wagon, the coroner produces a box of smaller masks and tosses one to each of us—and to each a pair of orange rubber gloves. We don the masks, making B-movie aliens of ourselves, laughable in the transformation. Scotty glares out through the little glass circles in his mask, an embittered earwig, all the more improbable for the twin shocks of white hair that protrude from either side of the centre strap of his proboscis.

The forensics people spread a heavy rubber sheet beside the grave, chat briefly with the coroner, then extract from their van a set of self-standing green curtains and set them up along two sides of the grave. Next comes a pair of floodlights that hum like cicadas and brighten the already glaring daylight.

With the stage set and the audience brimming, Peter descends into the pit. He peels back a small chunk of the sodden lid, then another about the size of a serving platter. At the instant the horrors beneath are about to be laid open, an alarm sounds in the back of my skull, and I whirl and walk hastily back from the brink. When I have taken four or five steps, Peter lets out an otherworldly yowl. Several groans and *O-gawds* burst muffled from behind gas masks, and within seconds, even at ten yards' distance, an unearthly smell has begun to seep into my mask— a fiery, caustic poison that burns the sinuses and convulses the stomach and lungs.

An agonizing minute later, Peter emerges with the grey-brown remains in his arms and lays them out on the rubber sheet before leaping from the grave and, as if chased by hornets, sprinting fifty yards out into the Garden of the Blessed Redeemer. As he comes to a halt, he rips off his mask, throwing his face skyward, sucking fresh air in rapid implosive gulps. Having steadied his breathing, he leans over, puts his hands on his knees and a few seconds later vomits quietly into the grass.

At the grave, the coroner's assistant and the forensics technicians squat by the corpse, poking and picking at it. In their masks, and with their bone saws and chisels, they resemble low-order carrion thieves, horror-movie creations, on some ghastly mission from the dark side.

I wander over to where Peter is flaked out on the lawn in the sweat-saturated shorts he has been wearing beneath his zip-up suit. Hogjaw is ministering to him with a tin cup and five-gallon pail of water, most of which Peter eventually dumps over his head.

Within half an hour, the forensics work is complete, and Scotty, as contrite as I have ever seen him, hobbles over, lifts his mask and asks Peter if he's ready for another go. "We'll wrap her in the rubber sheet," he says, his rolling *r*s betraying no sign whatever that he is forty years gone from the auld sod.

Peter re-girds and, with exaggerated strides, advances on the remains of the day.

When Gus is again in her grave, Peter rips off his suit, mounts the backhoe with an equestrian flourish, and blasts the carbon from its pistons and pipes. Meanwhile, the technicians and officials have packed up and are on their way, their stinking evidence hermetically stowed in dainty glass containers.

A few days hence, that same evidence—four or five bran flake–sized bits of lung, muscle and nerve tissue—will secure the case not for the Crown but for the defence and will play a significant role in the acquittal of Sprocket Bowness.

By 3:30, we are finished our work, each of us already in the process of sublimating its effects. Peter seems angry, while Luccio, well toked, is prattling non-stop about Sprocket Bowness; about the interdependency of sex and death; about marijuana as a cure-all for the ills of the world. Scotty has returned ahead of us to the shop to beef up his defences. But as we stagger in he makes an unexpected appearance and, in imperial fashion, orders us all home, with pay, for the remainder of the workday. "*Rrregular* pay," he reminds us, and like the others I am impressed by the gesture. Unlike them, I have little difficulty accepting it at face value.

"Some day next January," mutters Hogjaw, "when it's thirty below, in the middle of a blizzard, five minutes before quitting time, he'll come in here needing a road shovelled or ground broken, or something, and he'll grin and say 'Remember that day last summer when I gave you all an hour off?'"

"And you know what I'll tell him," interjects Peter. "I'll tell him, 'You're dreaming, Scotty! You never gave us an hour off! And if you did, we didn't take it! So we don't owe you a gawdam thing! And if you need somebody to shovel yer gawdam road, go out there to Holy Angels and get that stinker we pulled outta the ground for ya last summer—get *her* to help you shovel; have a drink with her while you're at it—you can get as drunk as you are right now!"

The rant ceases as suddenly as it began, and in its wake, a silence settles on the shack. The ritual removal of work boots and socks and the resulting stench (by comparison, as reassuring as lavender) is a kind of closure both on the temper and on the sensory assault of the past few hours.

"Tempus fugit!" says Luccio presently. "Enjoy your hour, boys—here's to Gus Bowness!" And he stands up and draws a tiny bag of grass out of his pants pocket.

And with that, we begin to savour our hour—stung, yes, but each a little giddy with the afternoon's haul of wages.

twelve

THE BUSINESS OF

BEING ALIVE

AS A KIND of purge—and a way of vapourizing some of our newly accumulated wealth—Luccio suggests that we go for a beer. We rattle down Kingston Road and pull up in front of a depressing little tap room with a rubblestone facade caked in decades-old filth. The atmosphere inside is not so much air as a sort of air-conditioned toxicity—cigar ash and brewery mould, the armpits and ass cracks of any number of old hopheads who have sat in the place over the years in a thousand variations on what is possible on the descent into the potter's field. Meanwhile, the day's other evil smell has penetrated my sinuses like tear gas, where it will remain for weeks. A couple of large drafts go some way to diluting it. A couple more, and the question of Luccio's work prospects enters the conversation, bringing an ironic smile and the languid pronouncement that his prospects have been downgraded to "last-ditch hopes." He tells me about a recent job interview—a surreptitious appointment for which he booked off sick—conducted by a bristling female personnel officer with Manufacturers Life Insurance. Their meeting ended, according to Luccio, with her comment that she never could have imagined herself interviewing a gravedigger for an assistant vice-presidency. "I told her," he says, "that what I was really doing at the cemetery for $2.30 an hour wasn't gravedigging but unscrewing the stiffs that her own company had made their billions screwing." Suddenly Van Morrison is wailing out of the jukebox about jasmine-smelling madams and the back streets of Dublin. Luccio slouches off to the washroom, his size-38 khakis drooping off his backside like a newspaper delivery bag. When he returns, he says, "If I were interviewing applicants for a job, I'd ask them two questions and two only: What's your favourite virtue? What's your favourite vice? And I'd hire them based on the honesty and imagination of their answers."

His own favourite virtues, he allows, are cruelty and laziness. As for vices, he cannot think of one he doesn't like—rattles off a litany of them that includes lust, gluttony, greed, vanity, duplicity . . . "and sarcasm!" he cries, "and irony!"

His roll call of preferred sins—"of indispensable human survival tactics"—catches the attention of a dissolute old man who throws a bony fist in the air and shouts, "Revenge!"

"To revenge!" responds Luccio, and he gestures with his glass and pours another six ounces of beer into his throat.

I ask about Imperial, from whom he says he hasn't heard in nearly a month. Almost beyond reason, he is still expecting a job offer of some sort—or at least another interview. If he doesn't have a job by October, he says calmly, he'll "pack up and head out—anywhere they need economists."

It is the first time I have heard him acknowledge that his time in the city may be waning. It is also the first time I have heard him refer to his intended profession without some self-deprecating scorn (in this lies the beginning of a dispiriting erosion of the humour and contempt that have sustained him through the early and mid summer). He says he'd consider Australia or New Zealand as destinations. "Or gawdam Burma or Borneo," he says. "Have shovel—seek bullshit."

Lucy, too, has had difficulties with Immigration, but according to Luccio she can stay right where she is, in that "technically" she is married to a Canadian.

"She's married?" I ask, momentarily bemused by the revelation.

"With full carnal knowledge," says Luccio.

"To who?"

"To *whom*," he says softly—the whom here being "a greasy little bridge troll" named Tony Bassacardo. "Tony the Bastard," intones Luccio—"Tony the black-assed Buzzard." Lucy apparently has not lived with the Buzzard in two years. But faithful to her Papist conditioning, she has never filed for divorce. "We grew up with the guy," says Luccio. "Then he came over here, and then Lucy came over." He takes a swig of beer and says, "I'd tell you the rest is history, Wilkins, but the rest is fucking bullshit. I have no idea why a good-looking young woman with brains would marry a lumpy little psychopath who walks around Montreal with a pepperoni in his pocket and sleeps with a nine-millimetre Beretta under his bed. The only book he ever read was the authorized biography of gawdam Benito Mussolini!"

FAR FROM disheartening me, these latest revelations restore a measure of gusto to my latent fascination with Lucy. For weeks, off and on, I have enjoyed low-key fantasies about her, as well as a recent dream—a gropey, tumescent affair, overridden by her fears, and perhaps my own, that we would be discovered by her father or brother or someone.

As Luccio and I get up to go, I suggest that we drive straight to North York, that we pick up Lucy, go out to eat and then get out of the city for the evening. While the depredations of the afternoon continue to go unspoken, there is for both of us a fairly obvious need to throw off the memory of Gus Bowness.

But as we rocket north up the Don Valley, the sense that liberating hours lie just ahead is temporarily tarnished by Luccio's grinding denunciation of Willowlawn and of his increasingly tenuous employment there. At one point, in the course of thirty seconds, he catalogues the place as "the sub-basement of the salt mines," and "a disgusting black hole" and "an alley to the arse end of eternity." Today, in addition to everything else, he has an ecological condemnation—the fact that the entire cemetery is what he calls "a stew pot" of formaldehyde from the embalming wars. "Then we douse the gawdam place with Agent fucking Orange so the dandelions won't grow!" He says he can't see why any self-respecting dandelion would want to live in such a place anyway. As for his secret plot of marijuana, he acknowledges that it is undoubtedly contaminated from the roots up—a sobering thought for one who has participated liberally in consuming it for nearly three months.

I remind him above the whine of the engine that, despite our shared antipathies toward the place, he obviously feels a lot worse than I do about it.

"I should fucking hope so!" he hollers back. "For you, it's a whistle stop—you might as well be working at the Red Barn! For me, it's the last gawdam thread between survival and extinction!" He reminds me that, unlike myself, he can't go home and "curl up" on his parents' rug, or borrow a week's wages—can't even get a visa to stay in the country. "Mr. Just-fucking-Society Prime Minister would rather see me in fucking prison in Quaddafiville!" Willowlawn, he laments, is "a godless fucking dead-drop . . . and every time I lay out a grave in the fucking place—in fact, every time, I'm reminded that people routinely spend more gawdam money on the embalmed stiffs of their so-called loved ones than I've ever had spent on me as a living human being…" By this time, he is poking me painfully on the thigh with the knuckle of his index finger, one good thump for every new complaint in his apparently endless litany. "Every time I do fucking *anything* in that gawdam place," he grimaces, "it's as if I have my face driven into the fact that I'm going gawdam fucking nowhere and going there fast!"

We do not speak again until we reach the 401. As we accelerate onto the freeway, he shouts, "We gotta eat!" and from somewhere on the ample tracts of his person he produces a KitKat bar and a banged-up joint. He buries his head in the lee of the windshield, sparks the reefer, then relaxes as the smoke twists from the corner of his mouth into the slipstream behind the car.

Lucy has been temporarily laid off at the flower shop where she has been working and is only too happy for the chance to get out of town for a few hours. She disappears into one of the bedrooms in her bathrobe and reappears a minute later in bell-bottomed jeans and a wispy cotton blouse, the tails of which are knotted beneath her breasts so as to accentuate their plumminess. Six inches of her midriff are showing, and a kind of mandala of a belt buckle sits two inches below her navel. There is a delicacy to her bone structure and bearing that is missing in Luccio, and yet like him she has a lustiness about her that seems somehow connected to the sea and vineyards and to the ripening peasant gardens on the terraces of coastal Calabria.

We linger over our meal at the Madison, an old-style deli whose specialties are Montreal smoked brisket and dill pickles no bigger than shotgun shells but mighty with garlic. The meat is addictive, especially to a pair of stoners, and unable to lay off, I tuck into a plate of it slathered with mustard so fiery that at first bite it brings tears to my eyes and sends white-hot needles up behind my nose.

By the time we emerge from the air-conditioned interior, the wind has dropped, the effects of the grass have gone punky, and the heat and mugginess seem burdened with the vapours of the afternoon. But in no time, we are sailing north on Highway 48, cooled by the rush of air through the open cockpit of the car. Lucy is scrunched up in the storage well behind the seats.

At Jacksons Point, on the south shore of Lake Simcoe, under pressure from Lucy to stop so that she can stretch her legs, we fetch up in front of a teetering wood-frame hotel, one of those fart-ridden peculiarities of Canadian hostelry that exists for no other reason than to sell beer, but for licensing purposes must offer a half-dozen rooms in which, say, a cemetery worker and a dark-haired adulteress could crash for the night after drinking themselves love-sick.

The owner, a former pro hockey star named Tod Sloan— "the Slinker," as he was nicknamed for his nifty skating and puck-handling—has ballooned to twice his playing weight, but is not so embarrassed by the reinvention that he hesitates to dec-orate the walls with framed photos of himself as a sinewy war-rior in the uniform of the Toronto Maple Leafs. Luccio hits it off with him and is soon regaling not only the Slinker but half a dozen regulars with graveyard stories. He is animated, he is aggressive, he is in his element. And those around him drink it all in as heartily and indiscriminately as they knock back their beer. They are fascinated particularly by accounts of the illegal unearthing of bones and of the recent strike, with its dashed stiffs and refrigerated ghosts. The stories are a kind of goad against the tedium and predictability of their lives, and as the beer bar-rels sweat and the twilight thickens beyond the windows, a spirit of barely sublimated violence is increasingly present in the room. Such a mood might be worrisome except for the presence of the 350-pound Slinker who, if not exactly in a position to stop a fight were one to break out, or even to move quickly down the bar or take a deep breath, is clearly respected by his clientele. There is also of course the presence of our own 240-pound equalizer who looks capable of performing an impromptu autopsy on any of his newly acquired bar buddies.

Meanwhile, Lucy and I sit at a table by the window, discussing the evolving chaos that is her life. What affects her most is that her friends are elsewhere—in Montreal, in Vancouver, in Rome. She has applied for work in an Italian travel agency, but with her limited education, all of it from back home, her opportunities too are limited. She is qualified to go to university, but is uncertain about four years of financial deprivation. Beyond everything, of course, her marriage is a farce—albeit a necessary farce as she gropes for stability. At the moment, the Buzzard is required by court order to give her fifty dollars a week in spousal support. While she is reluctant to admit it, her best hope is that Luccio will land a decent job, which would give them new digs and an improved foundation from which to operate. However, she has witnessed his struggles, has participated in them and isn't counting on anything.

Luccio continues to hold his gothic assemblage in thrall. Like Scotty, he is bullish on the cartoon horror not only of death but also of the industry that surrounds it. Unlike Scotty, he sees it all as a kind of echo of that other cartoon horror that is the business of being alive. As I approach to suggest that perhaps we should get moving, he is entertaining his fellow drinkers with an almost scholarly review of death and burial oddities—not just of the human species but in this case of the praying mantis, a long-legged insect the male of which cannot complete mating while its brain is attached to its body. For that reason, the female rips the male's head off when she has taken what she needs from him and simply flies away, leaving him brainless and thrashing. Luccio's comment on this apparent violation of nature is that it lends new meaning to the term "giving head," which brings forth a grunt of laughter, and another beer for the *bhopa*, the storyteller, the merry and morbid chronicler. As I stand within earshot, he tells them, among other tasteful tidbits, that before modern embalming, and particularly the invention of the stethoscope during the mid-1800s, comatose people whose pulses were undetectable to the touch were routinely buried as dead and occasionally regained consciousness, only to find themselves in the dark, underground, with extremely limited air. As a safeguard against such catastrophes, particularly where the rich were concerned, "cemeteries would rig a little bell with a rope on it that went down a tube into the coffin—I mean it!" he says. The grave keeper was paid to keep his ears open, and after a week, if he didn't hear the bell, would remove the tube. Taking barely a breath, the cemetery Socrates informs his circle of acolytes that the tradition of sending flowers to a wake originated before embalming, when, as he puts it, "stiffs routinely started to stink before they were buried"—for which reason they were laid out in rooms filled with the most fragrant blossoms available.

Luccio has yet to address the events of the afternoon, but I have an inkling he will not leave without doing so. Then, as if cued to my thoughts, he is onto it, into it, bringing an abrupt change of mood, as well as a new fascination, in that several of the leather-vested bikers know the murder case in question—in fact knew Gus Bowness, who, with Sprocket, was an occasional drinker at Tod Sloan's Hotel. In describing the afternoon, Luccio draws a baleful and disgusting image of the blackened corpse, of its vomit-inducing smell, and in so doing incurs the wrath of a young drunk, who plants himself under Luccio's nose, fixes him with a stare and says: "How do we know this ain't all bullshit?"

Under the circumstances, I might expect Luccio to call on me to corroborate. But he apparently feels no such need. Instead he steps back, glaring down impassively at his inquisitor. When the air between them is about to snap, he says quietly, "You don't, my friend. And if you think it is, you don't have to listen."

The tension is quickly diffused, but the spell, such as it is, has been broken, and not even the Slinker, with all his nifty moves, can put it back together.

HAVING DRUNK more than we should have, we meander back along the lakeshore in the darkness. At a strip of beach within sight of several cottages but secluded enough to be private at this time of night, we pull over. Luccio is determined to go swimming—claims he still has "the stink of the afternoon" on him—and is insistent that Lucy and I go with him. I follow them along the sand in the moonlight, into the shelter of a grove of willow trees, where without a word Luccio begins taking off his clothes. Lucy, too, is quickly down to her underwear, leaving me briefly transfixed and then scrambling to catch up. As poised as Athena, she pauses on the shoreline, so that Luccio and I are first into the sandy, tepid lake. When I am up to my shoulders, I turn and watch Lucy stepping gingerly toward me into the shallows. Luccio swims out, then returns, and for several minutes the three of us splash around in the waist-deep water. As we are about to get out, Lucy grabs my shoulders from behind. She is a good-sized woman, perhaps five-foot-nine, and by pulling me backwards she succeeds in driving me under, straddling me in such a way that as I regain my balance, I come up with my face lodged briefly between her thighs, and, as I attempt to push off, against her backside.

We dry off as best we can on the car blanket and, with Lucy again huddled in the smallish space behind the seats, I drive hard toward the city, my brain caught in a kind of comic-strip skid between the images of the past twenty minutes and a blossoming anticipation of what may be to come.

AT THE apartment, I follow Lucy and Luccio up the stairs, feeling suddenly like a preschooler who has tagged along with older kids in hopes of joining their play or copping a bit of candy.

Luccio makes toast in the kitchen and smacks it down with a can of sardines before muttering his good nights and disappearing into his bedroom.

Lucy allows me to kiss her in the living room and, when I attempt to move things along, takes my hand, draws me toward the couch, flops into the corner of it and pulls me down beside her. But when I allow my hand to settle lightly in her lap, she says quietly that she doesn't "think so," that Luccio wouldn't like it, although it is equally apparent that the Holy Mother, under whose unrelenting gaze she was raised and educated, wouldn't like it either, or for that matter the Son of the Holy Mother, or the Almighty Daddy—reminding me emphatically that Lucy's puissant adolescent honour, her vaunted Papist conditioning, make insignificant flyspeck of whatever desires she might hold for the likes of me. But my compulsion to get into her jeans (another honourable entitlement of the Almighty Daddy, or at least of His plan for the continuation of the race) is not easily rebuffed, and in a reprise of my own deep conditioning—which is to say bone-hard high-school persistence—I make a renewed attempt to draw her down beside me.

"No, no, no," she admonishes quietly, and with mildly contrived exasperation she sits up and straightens her blouse. The sound of traffic whooshes up from the street through the open windows. After several seconds, she takes my hand, pops a conciliatory kiss onto my cheek and leads me out onto the balcony.

We stand on the tiny pallet of concrete that passes for a front yard, leaning on the railing, looking across Avenue Road at fifty or so similar pallets.

"We could talk about it," she shrugs.

"About what?"

"You know," she says, and she repeats the weary little bluster that is her rationale for laying off sex, at least with me: that she is a married woman a dozen years my senior, that it is against her beliefs, that she doesn't think it would go over well with "Looch."

"Who's gonna tell him?" I ask, to which she arches an eyebrow but says nothing.

With the air thinning between us and my exhaustion settling, I no longer have it in me to press the point.

"Time to go to bed," she murmurs, stranding me briefly between her meaning and my own tawdry inference. "I mean to sleep," she laughs.

And indeed, within forty minutes, I am curled up asleep, not with Lucy, as I might have hoped, but alone, in air-conditioned discomfort, in the spare bedroom of my parents' east-end apartment.

Not surprisingly, the night is a twisted reinvention of the day, a state of turmoil in which every waking nuance is given another suffocating turn. Twice I am wrenched awake by dreams, the first of which has me trapped underwater with Lucy Pucci, who is painfully, tantalizingly naked and who is determined to show me that we can all live happily (sans swimsuits) beneath the surface of Lake Simcoe. To that end, she adroitly removes my rib cage, giving me greatly expanded lung capacity but leaving me as limp and powerless as a string.

Closer to dawn, Gus Bowness appears, standing at the foot of a grave in which I am stretched out in the vestiges of a coffin. She smiles; she breathes; she prevents the skin from slipping from her face. She is in need of a little comfort, she says, as she snuggles in beside me. In order to live forever, she explains, one must attempt to keep the blood in one's veins, the hair on the scalp, the teeth in the gums—one must attempt to keep the flesh on one's bones.

thirteen

THE IMPERFECT POSSIBILITIES

OF THE VENAL NEW WORLD

BY MONDAY morning, the report is in on Fred's illness—acute salmonella poisoning. Scotty has been to see him in the hospital over the weekend, where he was informed by a "nurrrse" that, had Fred not received emergency care when he did, he would have been dead within a day from dehydration. His blood pressure, Scotty says, was 25 over 20 when they brought him in, bragging that his own heroic BP was once as high as 170 over 110. He repeats the story to all and sundry as he sorts out the day's assignments, stressing the tale's obvious indications of his acuity in sending someone to check on Fred. At break, Luccio tells him about a legendary Italian nobleman who saved the life of one of his soldiers on the battlefield. "A year later," says Luccio, "the soldier went crazy and murdered the nobleman's wife and children."

"What are you saying?" snaps Scotty, "that I should have let him die—that now I've gotta watch out for my wife and children?"

"What I'm saying," says Luccio, "is that, for better or worse, if you save someone's life, you're responsible for everything the person does from that day forward."

"I'm glad I didn't save *your* gawdam life," says Scotty.

"And I hope I never have to save yours," says Luccio.

"Which makes two of us," responds Scotty, who, despite anything he might have been told at the hospital, has reduced the pathology on Fred's illness to two possible causes: consumption of raw chicken or consumption of raw eggs, both of which carry the salmonella bacteria.

Norman, paying at best partial attention and confused by the edible-sounding bacteria, demands to know why anyone would choose to eat raw salmon.

"For the same gawdam reason they'd eat raw chicken," Peter tells him.

"People eat raw chicken?!" exclaims David, emerging suddenly from his self-absorption.

By lunch hour a nasty wind has come up out of the east. The sky is as busy as a clothes dryer. Luccio and I race to Paletta's without taking time to put the top up on the Alpine. As long as we are moving, the windshield protects us from the spattering of rain. But at the stoplights it gusts in, prompting Luccio to reach into the storage compartment and fashion a crude sombrero out of yesterday's newspaper.

As we await our meatball sandwiches, Luccio phones Lucy and learns that his long-anticipated call from Imperial Oil—the cherished annunciation—has arrived, and that he is to phone a Mr. So-and-so that afternoon. He also learns that a letter has come from the *West Coast Review,* to which he has sent several of his stories. He orders Lucy to open and read it over the phone and stands there by the bar bouncing on his toes, inflating his chest, puckering and stretching his lips. Unable to erase the smirk from his unrepentant puss, he eventually smacks down the receiver and comes waltzing across the floor bleating that he is about to become a published writer. *"Vino economico!"* he shouts at Paletta, who, quickening to the whims of the newly anointed celebrity, reaches beneath the bar and produces a half-empty bottle of decidedly inferior table wine which he insists has been open "just a few days" and which he proceeds to divvy into a quartet of cappuccino glasses on the marble bar top. "Okay!" he says, raising his glass. "Here's to Mr. Big Shot! To our own Mario Puzo!"

After the ritual clinking and Luccio's vociferous complaints over the wine, Paletta, his face now a study in puzzlement, says quietly, "How much you gonna get, Lootch? How much they gonna pay you?" He is under the radically misguided impression that publication in an obscure Canadian literary rag is tantamount to an appearance on the *New York Times* bestseller list, perhaps even to the ultimate literary dream, which is of course to sell out to Hollywood. But Luccio backs him off with a wag of his finger, a warning not to sully the moment with thoughts of the embarrassing pots of coin that will unavoidably be involved.

"Yeah, yeah, I understand—you don't wanna talk about it," insists Paletta, speaking more softly and seriously now. "I just wanna know how much they gonna pay you."

"Half a million," snaps Luccio. "Is this the only gawdam wine you've got? Where's Maria? Get her out here for a toast!"

"Half a million *what?*" protests Paletta.

"Relax!" hollers Luccio. "It's literature! It's irrelevant!" He pauses, as if to pray, and informs Paletta that if he's lucky he'll get forty bucks for his story and a few copies of the magazine.

Relieved, Paletta shouts at his wife to "come make some toast—our friend Luccio's gonna make a book!"

"A *story!*" says Luccio. "One little story in one little magazine," and, for the benefit of his hosts, he describes it now, explaining the futuristic society in which everybody spends time in jail every year, etc., etc. "I wrote it in two hours," he says.

"Iss very good," intones Paletta, who has sat glassy-eyed through the telling but is determined to apply the stamp of recognition. "Iss worth way more than forty bucks."

"I'll sell it to you for whatever you wanta pay," brightens Luccio, and, in the light of Paletta's skepticism, explains to him how Turkish storytellers gather a crowd in the marketplace and, when their listeners are hooked on a story, will stop and demand another coin if the tale is to continue. "The better the story, the more the people pay."

Paletta, however, wants no part of any deal that would see him spending cash on anything as inconsequential as writing when it could be used to buy car tires or television sets or patio furniture. He declares now that he knows nothing about stories anyway—"unless ees by Alighieri or Boccaccio or something," he allows. He marks the names of the greats with a toss of his hand. "What I'm gonna do with a story by Luccio Pucci?"

"You could read it," suggests Luccio.

Paletta turns to me and asks if I think it's worth money. When I assure him it is, he is again seized by the spectre of Luccio oozing cash and flying off to Hollywood. However, he cannot quite equate such transcendence with Luccio's sketchy précis, or with his perversity or profanity—or of course his poverty, which Paletta, like most people who know Luccio, assumes is a function of everything else that makes him the lumbering nonconformist that he is. Nevertheless, if there is any chance that Luccio is to become the darling of the literary world, Paletta wants his own little piggy in the parade; and, with what remains of the rancid vinegar that he has been pouring as wine, he proposes a solemn toast to "the Dante *nuovo*" of the book world.

"You're far too kind," says Luccio.

"I'm a beliefer!" shrugs Paletta. "I belief you are a great author."

As we get up to go, Luccio returns to the phone and puts in his call to the personnel department at Imperial. His phone voice is that of a slightly indignant schoolboy.

His appointment is for Wednesday he tells me as we leave the restaurant. The job he is being offered is in Marketing and Finance.

"Doing what?" I ask, and without missing a beat he says he expects to waste most of his time fostering "an imaginary need for petroleum culture and products among unsuspecting third-world countries." It all connects somehow to the content and conclusions of his dissertation. "More importantly, Wilkins, I shall be attempting to bury them in sufficient irresolvable debt that the company, out of fiscal benevolence, will eventually have to go in and take charge of their mineral and gold reserves—and of course their temples and virgins; Imperial is above all a spiritual and sensual organization . . . Ha!" he shouts as he swings open the car door.

After a year at the cemetery, he is of course looking forward to the money, and as we beat it south on Don Mills Road, he relaxes in the passenger seat—head back, eyes closed, tongue on sabbatical—savouring the imperfect possibilities of the venal new world that is about to open before him.

fourteen

THE LAND OF LOW
EXPECTATIONS

BY EARLY afternoon, I am aware of a subtle but discernible difference in the atmosphere out in the Garden of the Immaculate
Conception where I am clipping hedges and watering shrubs.
It's as if there has been some inscrutable rise or fall in the humidity or atmospheric pressure. My discovery at coffee break that
Scotty has not been on the grounds since noon hour is convincing evidence of the degree to which his black Scottish spirit per-
vades even the farthest corners of the premises and affects the
entire drift of what goes on. He has apparently told Peter that he
has "personal" matters to attend to and that he'll be back at some
point during the afternoon. However, as we sit under the maples
drinking coffee and scarfing up butter tarts, Scotty's grandson
David reveals that the heat wave has been hard on his chroni-
cally ill grandmother, that she has taken a turn for the worse and
that Scotty is at home nursing her. The notion of Scotty playing nursemaid to his wife or anybody else, especially during the
afternoon when he is typically drunker than a chimp, hardly
goes down without a gulp. But under the circumstances, no one

makes light of the situation. Resisting open celebration of our deliverance, we mark the occasion by sparking a stubby reefer and taking a quadruply long break, quietly sanctioned by Peter who has filled his last grave of the day and is content to languish in the ninety-five-degree heat.

By the next morning, Scotty's wife has been installed in the East General Hospital.

Over the next few days, Scotty comes and goes, dragging himself up to his office, speaking rarely, and then only to issue the orders of the morning or afternoon.

Late Thursday afternoon as I am at work on a sinker in the Garden of the Blessed Redeemer, he stops along the road and gets out of his car, beckoning me toward him, demanding that I get him a "few cut flowers for Mrs. MacKinnon." His eyes, the usual litmus test of his drunkenness, are hidden behind his sunglasses. But there is a heavy boozy vapour around him, and it isn't difficult to see that he is all but dead drunk.

From a heap of new bouquets not a hundred feet away, I make up a summery-looking arrangement, mostly of lilies and snapdragons, and march it across the lawn to him. Meanwhile, he has commenced a muttering rant, a *sotto voce* diatribe . . . about Peter . . . about Hogjaw . . . about Luccio . . . about David and Al. For some reason, today, he is particularly exercised about those gentlest of cemetery inhabitants, the flower children, "the huppies," as he calls them, who wander in and out, smoking grass, strumming guitar, putting up a kindling fire after dark, and leaving behind the occasional wine bottle or condom, a little latex ode to the spirit and freedom of the age. "They raid the gawdam gardens!" he whines, the picking of live flowers long having been the most brazen and contemptible of cemetery transgressions. It seems probable that Scotty's real argument with the kids is less their violation of the gardens than of the larger world of A. "Scotty" MacKinnon—of compliance, of conformity, of repression, embodied most vigorously, it would seem, by what he assumes is their "non-stop appetite for the joy-stick" . . . or for joy, period . . . or for anybody or anything that is not as hopelessly inhibited and embittered as he. He has never quite shaken it from his skull that Peter or Luccio, or even his grandson, may be "in gawdam cahoots with them." But as his enfeebled protest plays itself out, it is clear that it has less to do with Peter or flower children or picked posies than with Scotty's own staggering frustrations. He teeters against the car, glances across its roof and says, "It's a wonder they haven't stole my gawdam tree!"

I beg his pardon, and he gestures up the road at the grand old Norway spruce by the statue of Christ at prayer in the Garden of Gethsemane, one of the most impressive trees on the property. "I planted it the year I got here," he says. "And if I had any gawdam sense, I'd chop the thing down—lay it right out there across the road! Gawdam graveyard doesn't deserve it!"

He creeps along the car, amidships, looks blankly at his watch and declares that he must get immediately to the hospital: "She'll be dead before I see her."

I venture to ask if he feels well enough to drive.

"Who else is there?" he demands as he slips behind the wheel, laying the recycled flowers delicately across the passenger seat. "Keep an eye on the Dutchman," he says through the open window, and having started his engine and double-checked the glove compartment, he does an awkward three-point turn, coming within a foot or so of knocking over a headstone. Then he heads up the road toward the north gate, a forlorn and fedora'd silhouette in the late afternoon sun.

EARLY ON Monday afternoon, Al Faragazzi, Willowlawn's raffish business manager, calls us together in the shop to tell us that Catherine McKinnon has "passed away."

Peter is placed officially in charge of the cemetery, and the flag, a tattered red ensign that flies from a wooden pole outside the entrance to the office, is lowered to half-mast. David accepts our condolences with an embarrassed shrug and wheels out of the cemetery on the deep-blue Kawasaki motorcycle that he has bought with his summer's earnings.

The afternoon goes smoothly, free officially of Scotty's influence, and at quitting time Al again appears in the shop. He is wearing a black lightweight suit, a black shirt and black python-skin cowboy boots. When he has collected us by the work-benches, he announces that he can get a deal on flowers if we're interested in sending a bouquet to the funeral parlour.

There is a silence, and Luccio says, "How good a deal?"

"Half price," says Al. "My sister-in-law's got a flower shop."

"Fine with me," says Hogjaw, but no one else says a word.

"Look," says Al after an uncomfortable silence, "I know you guys don't have a lot of money to be buying flowers, and I know damn well what most of you think of Scotty—I have my differences with him, too. But the guy *has* lost his wife. And I'll tell ya something—when any of your wives or kids have been in hospital and we've sent flowers from the management, Scotty's always put his money in."

Al looks briefly at his boots, then reaches for a cigarette, giving us more time than we need to consider his proposal. "Tell ya what," he says. "If you guys can scrape up ten bucks, I'll put in another ten, and we'll get some sort of a bouquet. You never know, it might heal some wounds."

"What's it to you, Al?" says Luccio.

"I'll tell ya what it is to me," says Al a trifle sternly. "A lotta people probably think I'm an asshole, and sometimes maybe I am. In fact, sometimes even *I* think I'm an asshole. I'm certainly not a guy to waste tears or get my violin out. But I happen to know that the old man hasn't got a lotta friends and that he isn't likely to get a whole lotta support or flowers. So I took it upon myself to stir up a little interest out here and in the office. Some of the salesmen and a couple of the girls are going to the funeral home tomorrow."

"Oh, for krisakes!" blurts Peter. "It's a buck each!" And with this there follows a grudging consensus that any man who has lost his wife—*any* man, it is stressed, so as to depersonalize the matter as much as possible—deserves an arrangement of (half-priced) flowers.

"Is everybody in agreement then?" asks Al.

As if submitting to a treatment that may well be worse than the disease, we allow that we are.

"Whaddaya want on the card?" says Al.

"May you and Scotty meet again soon!" deadpans Hogjaw, which draws a laugh, even from Al.

"How about 'In Deepest Sympathy'?" suggests Al.

"How about 'In Sympathy,'" says Peter, and we agree on "In Sympathy" and ante up a total of $10.30, which Al pockets before tooling out of the cemetery in his black LeSabre.

A MINOR act it may be, but Peter's speaking up for flowers—the reluctant transcendence of his grievances—is the beginning of his tenure as a man of responsibility at Willowlawn. As early as the following day, it is evident that he has surmounted the impatience with which he normally handles any sort of managerial chores and is ready to assume a mantle of low-key authority. Scotty's wife's funeral and burial are to take place on Wednesday morning, and late Tuesday Peter assembles us on the lawn outside the shop and lays out the plan for the interment. He does this so entirely without cynicism or rancour that his long-time contempt for the man might seem to be nothing more than a false memory or a piece of unmasked revisionism. In all likelihood, Al has taken him aside and instructed him that if he's going to be a manager, it would behoove him to start acting like one.

Peter's instructions for the funeral are that everyone is to bring a change of clothes, so that we're all properly dressed. He says, "Do you know what properly dressed means, Norman?"

"I don't own a suit."

"Do you own a tie?"

"Nope."

Peter says he'll bring him one, to which Norman responds that he's never worn one and won't know how to tie it, although he confides to me afterwards that he did once wear a tie when he was fourteen and had to appear in court charged with stealing his first set of drums. "Had to pay for them anyway," he says. "List! Could'a got 'em wholesale if I'd paid for them in the first place."

As we leave the shop, he delivers an impromptu history of his band, which began under the name ShitStick, became Bobby Gimby's Worst Nightmare, which, for fear of legal action, became Handel's Worst Nightmare, and is now Handel's Nightmare.

Why Handel?

"Because Handel can't sue us," says Norman, who as we reach the shop informs me that, tomorrow, for the burial, he has a special "dress" garment that he bought in Buffalo at Easter. If my understanding is correct, it is a long-sleeved black T-shirt printed in front to resemble a tuxedo: white bib, red bow tie, pearl buttons—to Norman's mind, decidedly respectful attire for the burial of the boss's wife.

The following morning, we report in not carrying but wearing our best bib and tucker. Hogjaw and Peter go immediately to the locker shed and exchange theirs for their usual rags and coveralls. But some of us linger briefly in our finery, as if the grubby labours before us might somehow be transformed in the natty glow of our threads. Luccio is wearing a double-breasted navy pinstripe, Italian-made, clearly of good quality, with hand stitching around the lapels. He has on a pale mauve shirt, with collar points the length of penknives, and a wide paisley tie. He is clean-shaven and looks less like a wage donkey than the well-read economist he is. Norman, as expected, is wearing his Buffalo commemorative tux, decidedly faded and so shrunken from washing that the sleeves stop four inches above his wrists.

At first glimpse of him, Peter screams across the yard, "Either get the fuck home and get a proper shirt or take the day off—in fact, get the fuck home or take the rest of the summer off!"

Since Norman lives miles from the cemetery and comes by bus, I volunteer to return to my parents' apartment at noon to get him a shirt. At home, however, I can find no suitable item in my closet, so abscond with one of my father's professionally laundered Van Heusens, size sixteen-and-a-half.

In the meantime, Peter has dug the grave, and Hogjaw and Luccio have assembled the props and accoutrements with slavish attention to their cleanliness and placement. Hogjaw has gone so far as to vacuum the rugs of Gratzenturf that are draped onto the walls of the grave and over the mound of fresh displacement.

Half an hour before the funeral is expected, we retire to the locker shed, remove our work clothes and, without so much as wiping our sweaty necks, get back into our dress duds and go out to the grave to make last-minute adjustments. As it turns out, my father is three sizes bigger than Norman, so the shirt hangs like an unstaked tent off his bony shoulders and spine. Nevertheless, he tucks it into his pants and attaches the tartan clip-on bow tie that Peter has brought for him (the tartan, by coincidence, being the battle colours of Scotty's most ancient tribal enemy, the Frasers).

Al needn't have worried about a shortage of flowers. Every funeral home in the city's east end has sent a sumptuously gaudy arrangement—sprays, "cushions," baskets. As we unload them, I spot our own cut-rate posy, an open spray of yellow gladioli and chrysanthemums, am in fact impressed to see it holding its own among bouquets that must have cost three times as much.

Eventually, a small procession of limousines and cars rolls down the main road, every headlamp glowing in the afternoon light. At the same time, from the direction of the back gate, barely glimpsed, a figure in a dark jacket and pants appears on a bicycle, peddling unsteadily toward us through the afternoon haze. I watch briefly through the dappled sunlight and leaves, then turn my attention to the main event, the arriving parade of mourners and pallbearers. But there are not as many of them as might have been expected by the abundance of flowers. Apart from ourselves, the office staff and a few local funeral home reps, there are perhaps a dozen or so family members and friends, David among them, looking ill at ease in his cheap suit, aiming the occasional self-conscious smile in the direction of his co-workers. As the pallbearers approach, carrying a small walnut coffin, I glance back, curious to see who has come by cycle and am jarred to see limping toward me a one-armed stick-man, an apparition so emaciated and pale that anyone would think the grave had been dug for him.

"Fred!" I blurt involuntarily, and Peter, Hogjaw and the others look round, each as surprised as I to see our one-time accomplice looking so spent and frail. Barely able to support the weight of his suit, Fred is nonetheless grinning broadly, apparently happy to see us and to be back in the land of low expectations. And as his fellow minions, we are delighted to have him back. Luccio pats him on the back, knocking him forward several inches and almost onto his face. When we have all shaken hands with him and adequately complimented his good health and vigorous appearance, we draw him into our midst.

Meanwhile, another familiar figure has worked his way to the graveside, apparently oblivious to everything around him. His eyes are red and moist, and his lower face, a pale mask of sagging wax, appears to have been suspended by hooks from the inner band of his fedora. Like Fred, he is a fossil, a bag of bones, and his black suit has clearly been bought for a more robust version of himself. Whatever life is left in the old sinner is flagged by his green tartan tie, the vestige and symbol of his mulish survivalist clan.

Scotty sobs sporadically through the committal of his wife's body, and seems about to swoon when he and the rest of us are revived by the unexpected rise of a confident contralto voice: *What a friend we have in Jesus . . . all our sins and griefs to bear . . .*

The singer is a marvelously leggy young woman in a black minidress with transparent sleeves and a voice so sweet that by the time she finishes there is hardly a dry eye around us (and among my peers, I suspect, hardly a cell of unexploded erectile tissue). Barely a minute passes before she embarks on an equally compelling rendition of the old Bing Crosby hit, a favourite of Scotty's, "When the Blue of the Night (Meets the Gold of the Day)."

After a closing prayer, there is an announcement that a lunch will be served at the home of Scotty's daughter, David's mother. Scotty, half-supported by a younger man and woman, one at each arm, stares at the coffin, his shoulders heaving periodically. In their turn, the pastor and several relatives greet him quietly, nodding their reassurances. However, as he starts toward the cars, he turns and, apparently for the first time, notices us standing in the background, shuffling self-consciously. He breaks away and shambles toward us, mouth agape, eyes focused somewhere behind and beyond. It is as if he has recognized acquaintances from another life, a previous incarnation, but cannot quite bring them into focus. We stand transfixed as he approaches, half-expecting a rebuke. Surely there is some minor imperfection in the laying out of the grave, some stray blade of grass encroaching on the integrity of the service. Or is it impertinent that we should be here at all, dressed like stooges, while the pay clock ticks in our favour and the cemetery goes to seed?

When he is close enough that we can smell the Scotch on his breath, he chews briefly on his dentures and is about to divest himself of the awaited message when he spots Fred and cries, "Good Lord Jesus Almighty, Fred! What's happened to ya? There's nothing left of ya!"

Fred, moved by the greeting, reaches out to Scotty and, in a scene that might have been lifted from some tawdry vaudeville melodrama, the two of them fall together sobbing. For several seconds, the one-armed scarecrow and the emotionally stunted old drunk hold feebly to what is left of the other, then pull back and regard one another in a rheumy, woeful stare. "Catherine's gone!" blubbers Scotty. "But you've been spared, Fred!" And without another word, he stumbles off toward a waiting limousine, irresistibly drawn by the green-bottled cure-all that undoubtedly awaits him beneath the seat.

HAVING CHANGED our clothes, we plug and tidy the grave while Fred watches silently from the shade. Despite the months of squalid speculation about Scotty and his kin and the violations that would be visited upon their graves, there are no shenanigans with the outer vault or coffin—no spray paint, no dickey birds, no grope for a token piece of jewellery. Indeed, when Peter has finished on the digger, he orders Hogjaw to hand-rake the soil, a rare and reverential procedure intended to remove the stones and bust up the lumps before the sod is rolled back into place. Peter himself eventually hauls the three-hundred-pound lawn roller back and forth over the grave, an act of almost obsequious respect, at least insofar as it pertains to grave-making at Willowlawn.

As we walk up to the shop, Fred pauses several times to examine the gardens, which to my mind are as fertile and lovely as ever. But he is clearly not pleased with the faint symptoms of dissolution that have settled in his absence: a withered blossom that should have been plucked, a spot of leaf blight no bigger than an oat flake, a square inch of garden soil unwatered since the teeming rains of twenty-four hours ago. What really sets him muttering is the sight of a ten-inch dandelion, rocketing up through the soil like Satan's prong, among his meticulously tended grandifloras and floribundas.

We sit on the lawn by the change shack, where Luccio fires up a reefer. We scarf up our sandwiches and celery sticks, offering Fred occasional nibbles. But he is careful about his intake, revealing (through Peter's translation) that he has eaten nothing but chicken broth for two weeks.

"Go bag hostipple," he says. "Go bag innamay." Evidently he has been released from the East General, and is to return there the following day.

At a lull in the lunch chatter, I tell Fred through Peter that it was I who came to his home when he was sick, and called an ambulance. "Yah, yah, goot for 'em," he nods, as he nibbles on a muffin that Hogjaw has given him. "I'm thengk you."

For the occasion of the funeral, he is wearing a tattered beige homburg with a grosgrain band, which gives him a jaunty, almost fashionable appearance, although, in his shrunken condition, it seems almost too much weight for his bony head and neck.

I get Peter to ask about Fred's family, those in the photographs, and listen as Peter threads his way through the translation.

"Yah, yah. Take 'em all dead now," says Fred, explaining that his wife and children were lost in an attempted flight out of Poland. He says he weighed "eighty ounces" when the Americans liberated him from a labour camp in Austria in 1945. He shows little emotion, the deeper of his feelings apparently long buried in survivalist stoicism. He presses the remainder of the muffin into his mouth, reaches into his loose cotton shirt and extracts a chain that hangs around his neck. On it dangles a tiny gold likeness of an elephant with its trunk raised, one of the universal symbols of the international circus.

"I am joggler," he says, and laughs ruefully. "Nats kill'em djoo; Nats kill'em jibseh; Nats kill'em blag; Nats kill'em sirka men—all kill'em kill'em." He cradles the tiny elephant in his palm, stares briefly down his nose at it and tucks it back in his shirt.

Five years would pass before I would read by chance and properly understand that the Reich's gassing of hundreds of itinerant clowns and circus performers was born of a fear that the performers' tenacious sense of independence was as threatening to Aryanism as were the Jews, gypsies and blacks.

Fred and his family had been jugglers and circus acrobats, at least a token of which information might have been known to us had Fred not lost an arm and, with it, the capability to present even a vestige of his lost skills.

In the dreamlike absence of any satisfactory response, we sit gazing into the grass or into the branches of the trees, caught somewhere, as usual, between the larger flow of forces and the more immediate diversions of the afternoon.

fifteen

NO MORE BULLSHIT

THE REMAINDER of the week is the usual low-key shuffle of clock-watching and evasions, as the temperature drifts back into the nineties. David returns to work earlier than expected, prompting speculation that he has come back to spy for his grandfather. The truth is that David is a more useful spy deployed *against* his grandfather than by him, and moved by the silliness of the notion that he is working against us, Peter tells us at assignment call that if that's what anyone thinks, he should challenge David on it, bring it out in the open. Of course, no one could do so without stopping to consider that David has, all summer, been a solid job companion, whose foremost allegiances have clearly not been to his grandfather. So, we let it pass, although Hogjaw, who has been ornery of late, refuses to work with David.

Only one funeral appears on each of Thursday and Friday, and, in Scotty's absence, the optional Saturday-morning shift—an occupational lull at the most demanding of times—becomes four hours of indolence, interspersed with the briefest of impulses toward grass clipping or stone cleaning or readying the tools for these inconsequential activities.

Luccio and I have volunteered for the shift, and as we play out its final minutes in the relative succour of the shithouse, Peter's voice sounds from the end of the path, calling us to a meeting in what has always been the most daunting of cemetery destinations, Scotty's office. Ill-omened and musty, the place is nonetheless a tantalizing locale for those of us who have, at most, spent a minute or two there, locating reading material or getting instructions or keys, but have never had the chance to idle amid the rubble, exploring desk drawers, boxes and old secrets.

Luccio and I ascend to find Peter sitting with his work boots on the desk, his heels grinding burial documents that, a week ago, would have been accorded the inviolability of sacred text.

Hogjaw is crouched by the window, sifting through an old whisky carton that contains, among other items, brooches, necklaces, spectacles, bracelets, rosary beads, plus an assortment of false teeth and bone fragments and what appear to be the workings of an old alarm clock.

"Si'down," says Peter, and we settle our backsides against the nearest convenient props—in my case a pile of dusty jute bags that I'm told were brought to the cemetery thirty years ago to haul carrots and potatoes out of the Victory Gardens that all but dominated the place during the war.

"When's the old man coming back?" Luccio asks quietly, to which Peter responds that he has no idea, but that the decision is no longer purely Scotty's. "Al and the rest of them are gonna decide next week."

For the moment, says Peter, he has a problem, and he directs his gaze at Luccio and me. "I need a worker—either of you know anybody who needs a job till the end of the summer?"

He slides a pair of completed employment applications onto the desk. "One of them's a broad," he says.

"Hire her!" says Luccio.

"I will if she's still around," says Peter, explaining that he intends to wait a day or two "to see if the old man shows up." Apparently, Scotty has already rejected the application.

Meanwhile, another problem has unearthed itself, in the form of a chastening realization that of the four of us only Luccio is adequately medicated for the drab methodologies of deadsville. To remedy this oversight, Luccio fishes up a bag of his private cure-all and twists a stout little plug, which emits an audible pop as he sparks it, sending an exploded seed and a thread-like rooster tail eighteen inches into the room. As smoke billows forth, Peter reaches over and opens the window so as not to contaminate entirely the vestiges of Scotty's administrative legacy. But for the most part, the sweet acrid smoke is allowed to linger, nourishing talk and laughter and camaraderie, which as much as the smoke are a kind of purge on the innards of the building. We sit rapt, as Richard Manuel bawls his spectral "Tears of Rage" from the speakers of Scotty's Blaupunkt radio, which for the first time in its life is tuned to CHUM FM. The Band is the featured entertainment of the hour, and delivers a succession of perfect moments via the cumulative brilliance of *Music from Big Pink*.

"So what are ya gonna do?" Hogjaw eventually intones above the strains of "Caledonia Mission."

Seconds pass before Peter says, "If you're talking to me, what am I gonna do about what?"

"About the girl," says Hogjaw.

"As soon as I find out who's boss, I'm gonna phone her up."

Hogjaw says if it were him, he'd phone the girl right now.

Peter, in no mood to be second-guessed, says immediately, "It *is* you, Hog! It *is* you this time!" and he picks up Scotty's black phone, turns it toward Hogjaw and thumps it to the front of the desk. "Here's the number," he says, pushing the girl's application over the desktop with sufficient force that it sails off and lands on a pile of old newspapers.

When there is no haste to retrieve it, I lean forward, pick it up and pour my distorted attention into its meticulously handwritten lines:

Name:	Denise Elizabeth Chartraw,
	705 Donlands Ave., East York, Ontario.
Phone:	755-1244
Birth date:	December 18, 1951
Dates available:	June 10–Sept. 4
Hobbies:	drawing, reading, drama, clarinet,
	travel (Expo 67, England)
Previous work	
experience:	– babysitting (since 12)
	– housekeeping
	– camp counsellor, Pioneer Camp,
	summer, 1968
Reason you	
want to work	
at Willowlawn:	Because I think it would be a very
	interesting place of employment, and
	because I enjoy working with people.

AS I absorb this unfettered testament to innocence, "Lonesome Suzie," another Manuel rainmaker, seeps from the radio speakers. I mention to those present that Denise Elizabeth Chartraw would like to be an employee of Willowlawn because she "enjoys working with people."

"She'll get over it," says Luccio.

But Peter, with his evolving attitude toward management, is intrigued. "Call her up!" he declares, practically throwing the phone at me, and fifteen seconds later I have Denise Chartraw herself on the line, an articulate teenager with an enthusiasm for graveyards that would suggest less than full perspective on her future at the bottom of the employee ladder at Willowlawn Everlasting. I explain to her, as Peter has instructed, that if she wants a job for the rest of the summer, she is to meet Peter at the shop at eight Monday morning.

Asking not a question about hours or pay or duties, she accepts the position, promising to throw over her babysitting gig for the pleasures of grave setting, brown patrol and the like. What she does not yet know is that, in accepting the job, she is to be Willowlawn's first female employee—at least the first actually to make graves. (Even now, there are two pathologically embittered non-men who have worked in the office since Shakespeare was a soda jerk and will continue to do so until they are laid to rest—let us say "unlaid" to rest—in their complimentary plots, in their rubberized girdles, in their prayerful hopes that existence beyond the veil will be free entirely of the human testicle-bearer, or at least the unpalatable notion of any sort of contact with the beast.)

Fortunately, we the corporate standard-bearers know well that Denise will be the first, and Luccio celebrates the occasion with a fresh reefer and an expressed hope that the new member of our tight-knit service unit will be fluent in philosophy and classical Italian . . . and the operas of Puccini . . . and of course the tonality of El Greco and the sensuality of Modigliani and Schiele.

As I drive Luccio to his bus stop, I catch a glimpse of red foliage in the row of soft maples along the north boundary of the cemetery and, as quick as that, am struck by a thought that we should get out of the city, take off for Muskoka, where I spent my boyhood summers at Port Carling. Norman has been bruiting it around since Wednesday that, because of a scheduling screw-up, Handel's Nightmare has been handed tonight's warm-up gig at The Kee in Bala. My curiosity is up, and Luccio, in spite of his contempt for Norman, is gleeful at the thought of escaping the city and spending a couple of nights in lake country. Besides, a bit of a toot is in order. If Luccio lands his job mid-week, we are unlikely to see him again at Willowlawn, the reality of which is just beginning to dawn on me. It is he of course who has given leavening and texture to my summer—I have been an hourly beneficiary of his seditious and literate imagination. He is, he once told me, an heir of Descartes, who, at the dawn of the European Enlightenment, required that all perceived knowledge be subjected to new and rigorous examination—"to ruthless objective scrutiny," as Luccio describes it. "No more bullshit."

While it is hardly an echo of the Age of Enlightenment, Luccio tells me as we drive that if he ever discovers the key to manipulating time, he will erase forever the sixteen months that he spent on the diseased soil of Willowlawn.

I remind him that the cemetery has given him the time to write his stories, and he laughs and says, "One thing I like about you, Wilkins, is your refreshing lack of perspective. But if you'll allow me to tell you something that might do you some good, it's that nobody *ever* gives you the time to write your stories or do anything else that might push a brick off the endless fucking conveyor belt. If you're going to get them written, you *take* the time."

We drive a block or two in silence, mildly wasted and now half-starved from the marijuana. "The problem," says Luccio as we rattle up Millwood Road, "is that most people would rather *sell* their time, or *kill* it, than nail it to the fucking wall. You know about that," he says, "you're a writer." The comment is a less-than-flattering reference to the half-dozen music reviews that I have written for the U of T newspaper, *The Varsity*, and that Luccio has seen and disparaged with all but gleeful condemnation (they are "immature," they are "hackneyed," they are "ill-informed").

We stop at his apartment and it occurs to me to call Peter to wheedle an extra half day, so that we do not have to be back until

Monday lunchtime. The drawback, if there is one, is that we will not get to witness the Stiff City debut of Denise Elizabeth Chartraw.

MY HOPE all along has been that Lucy might hop in the car and come with us. But she has gone to Montreal to meet her ex-husband—*"Il Maestro Mortadella!"* intones Luccio as he emerges from the bedroom with a pillow and overnight bag. "It's either divorce or they're getting back together."

For the moment, the thought of Lucy reuniting with someone whose erectile apparatus has earned him the nickname Maestro Mortadella—a man Luccio now tells me is fifteen years her senior—casts another layer of shadow over my fading fantasies about her. We exit the building into the parking lot, where the sun and wind, not to mention the weed, are suddenly a little less amenable.

However, the drive north on Highway 400 is in its own way a bracer, and as the traffic clears north of Highway 9, we are again, it seems, drifting downstream—for now at least into the pleasures of the weekend.

We stop at Webers for cheeseburgers and milkshakes and, still ravenous, pick up a four-quart basket of blueberries at a roadside stand, shoving the berries into our mouths in handfuls. It is nearly four o'clock when we arrive in Bala. With time on our hands, we boot it over to Port Carling and sack out under the white pines by the boat locks in the middle of town. Luccio rolls a reefer and, his imagination stoked, embarks on a detailed reminiscence about his boyhood summers in the hills around Siderno on the Italian coast of the Ionian Sea. It was during the summer of his seventeenth year, he confides, that his forty-year-old neighbour, a married woman, took him to her bedroom while her husband was off working the tomato terraces, massaged him with olive oil and introduced him to what he calls "the exhilarations of human duplicity." The sex ended, he says, when a door slammed a level below, and Luccio, naked and slick with oil, leapt out a window, landing knee-deep in manure in the cattle stables beneath the house.

An hour later we are back in Bala, and an hour after that are pressing into the dancehall with perhaps a thousand teenagers, most of them wearing black T-shirts and what would seem to be irreversible scowls. By the time we get inside, Handel's Nightmare is several numbers into its simple, deafening performance. The stage area is crowded and, from a distance, in the darkness of the hall, I believe I see Norman plunking it out on what appears to be a bass guitar.

We edge toward the stage, reaching it as the band finishes a mediocre cover of "Ruby Tuesday."

As the lights come up briefly on the stage, I see I'm mistaken, that the bass player is not Norman but a convincing look-alike, a kid with every one of Norman's features, including his pimples. I manoeuvre to the back corner of the stage, catch the kid's attention and ask if Norman Post is around.

"He's around here somewhere."

"He's not playing?"

"He's our equipment guy!" yells the kid as the first warped strains of "Green Onions" explode from the speakers.

We stand like mannequins for a few seconds, and five minutes later are seated in the bar of the Bala Bay Lodge, where for the better part of three hours Luccio refuses to talk about Norman or even to speak his name.

At midnight, in need of resuscitation, we drive to a little park on the Moon River for a swim, then on to Port Sandfield, where we come within a hair's breadth of side-swiping a pickup truck at the lift bridge. Our goal is Elgin House, an aging resort built during the palmy days of Muskoka Evangelical Revivalism. But it is now a mere dude ranch for affluent escapees from Michigan and Ohio and Pennsylvania. A staff party is supposed to be going on, but after cruising the property for ten minutes we have located nothing that suggests a celebration.

We drive off into the darkness, stopping two hundred yards down the road at the Elgin House golf course, where we spread our sleeping bags in a grove of pines and settle in for the night.

Luccio rises and fetches aspirins out of the glove compartment of the car. As he reappears out of the darkness I inquire lazily about his thoughts on Norman, to which he responds by asking if I have an extra sweatshirt.

"Not that'd fit you."

"For a pillow," he says, and I stumble upright and retrieve my high-school basketball jacket from the trunk of the car.

"May the revolution feed your children," he mumbles as he stuffs it beneath his head.

I lie staring into the night sky, stitching up the constellations, drifting deeper and deeper into space. A pinpoint of yellow light, perhaps a satellite, arcs across the firmament.

At sunrise, Luccio crawls from his bag fully clothed, looks around and says, "Where am I gonna crap?"

"Wait'll we get to town."

"I can't."

"In the bush."

He walks to the car, grabs some tissues, and marches onto the seventh green, where, declaring that golf is a bourgeois pastime for flabby capitalists like himself, he removes the flag, unzips his pants and squats above the cup.

WE SPEND Sunday in and out of the bar at the Bala Bay, and in the late afternoon run into a high-school classmate of mine, Jane Dickerson, the spoiled daughter of a prosperous Toronto electrical contractor. Jane's claim to notoriety at East York Collegiate, where we shared a desk in physics class, is that on Good Friday,

1966, she split a quart of lemon gin with her friend Laura Tammis and drove her dad's restored 1951 Packard over a sixty-foot embankment into the oaks and maples of the Rouge River Valley. In a back-seat incident a couple of months later she bit Brian Normandale, another of my classmates, so hard on the genitalia (apparently accidentally) that it took surgery to save the wreckage.

"Hey!" she screams as she sees me across the bar, and is immediately heading our way, giving Luccio the once-over as she approaches the table.

I order a round, and ten minutes later Jane jumps to her feet and invites us to her parents' cottage at nearby Acton Island.

We follow her in the car and, having crossed the narrow causeway onto the island, pull up at a grand old Muskoka mansion. Inside, Jane pours ample sloppings of her dad's cognac and warns us repeatedly that if her parents show up we should tell them we are friends of her brother David. She divulges without elaborating that she's had enough trouble for one summer already.

The cognac bottle drained, Luccio rolls a reefer, and we move onto the verandah, where, under the distorting authority of the smoke, we engage in an erratic discourse on our respective views of what our host refers to as "the nature of reality."

"What the hell's the difference between the *nature* of reality," demands Luccio, "and just plain reality?"

"The nature of it defines it," she fires back, stirred by his challenge to her semantics.

"If anything in the gawdam world defined *itself,*" says Luccio, "I'd think it might be reality!"

"Are you saying it can't be thought out?"

"What I'm saying," says Luccio, "is that just because *you* can't think it out doesn't mean nobody can."

Jane, who like me has completed two years of physics and philosophy at the University of Toronto, is wearing a skirt that might better be described as a see-through sash, so that Luccio and I, regardless of the abstractions of the debate, remain well focused on the material plane.

Eventually, she asks if I'm working, and when I tell her I'm at the cemetery with Luccio, she wants to know immediately if we ever see the bodies.

"Sometimes."

"Do you ever touch them?"

"I have," I tell her, and explain that one day recently a woman at an interment asked if I would open her dad's coffin and retrieve a railway watch from the old man's vest.

"And you did it?"

"Of course."

"Have you ever touched a woman—I mean a dead one?"

"Never."

"Have you ever touched a young woman?"

"Never touched any of them." However, I tell her about the body of the young woman who lay in the chapel for ten days during the strike.

"How do you know she was a young woman?"

"The undertaker told me."

"Did you see her?"

"Of course he did," says Luccio.

"Did you touch her?" Jane asks.

"I didn't even look at her!"

"A bit sensitive, are we?" chirps Luccio.

"Did *you* see her?" I ask him.

"What if I did?"

"Did you touch her?"

"What if I did?" he says.

"I'd have touched her," says Jane.

"Where would you have touched her?" says Luccio.

"I would have touched her where she needed touching," she

says quietly. She pulls on her cigarette, looks at me and says, "There's nothing wrong with touching the dead."

"Not my thing," I tell her.

"Oh, bullshit!" she says. "You looked in that coffin, didn't you? And you looked in it because it was a young woman."

If I am momentarily silenced by this turn in the spirit of the discussion, it has less to do with Jane's scolding than with the fact that I did indeed take a peek in the young woman's coffin— and for exactly the reason Jane has postulated, that it was the body of a young woman.

"Okay, I did," I tell her. "So what?"

"Did you touch her?"

"I didn't."

"Have you ever been turned on by a dead person?" she says.

"*Yeeeahhh!*" hoots Luccio.

"I don't know what you're getting at."

She says, "When my cousin died in a car accident, I'd never even noticed he was sexy. After he died, I stared for twenty minutes at him in the funeral home—then couldn't stop staring at this beautiful photo of him. He was the sexiest thing I'd ever seen."

As she speaks, my skull flushes a memory of my having been fascinated by the death of Marilyn Monroe and how the spread of photos that appeared in the *Toronto Star* catalyzed for me a year-long fantasy the likes of which I would not know again.

"Marilyn Monroe," I tell them.

"Ha!" screams Luccio. "So you're a necrophiliac after all! You boned her in spirit."

Before Jane can weigh in, furthering my reputation as a Casanova among stinkers, headlights appear in the lane beyond the cottage, and a minute later Jane's parents enter by the back door. They are a cartoon of affluent Muskoka cottage owners, from the golf hats to the Lacoste shirts to the pressed Bermuda shorts. As they enter the living room, Luccio and I stand to greet them.

"We'll get going," I tell Jane.

"Don't leave on our account," says her mother.

"They've gotta work in the morning," says Jane, who ushers us out the door and on up the lane to the car.

"Sorry about that," she says as we settle in.

I tell her I'll call.

"Do," she says, and as I start the engine, "You can show me around the graveyard some night."

"We'll dig one specially for you," says Luccio.

"You're sweet," she whispers, and we rattle off up the lane in reverse.

FIFTEEN MINUTES later, we are crashed out in an eight-dollar room at the Bala Bay Lodge, blowing a reefer to ease our descent into the lumpy pre-war mattresses.

Breakfast is a sordid affair consisting of pink-iced shirt cardboard, whimsically presented as Kellogg's Raspberry Pop-Tarts, and a chaser of instant oatmeal, made deliberately runny so that it can be ingested without milk or spoons.

With the car-top down and Smokey Robinson and Aretha Franklin pouring from the radio at 120 decibels, we race down Highway 400, managing to reach Willowlawn, as we had promised Peter, just before 1 P.M.

From a distance, at break, I catch a glimpse of Luccio and Norman converging on the snack truck from opposite directions. With a presentiment that I might be useful as a mediator, I hoof it toward them, arriving in time to hear Luccio ask Norman how the gig went in Bala.

"Great!" says Norman, momentarily taken aback by Luccio's unexpected interest. "Eleven hundred people—you shoulda been there."

"We were there," smiles Luccio. "Wilkins and I."

"I mean you shoulda been in Bala."

"We were in Bala."

"On Saturday night?"

"On Saturday night."

"You were in Bala on Saturday night."

"We were in Bala on Saturday night."

A look of bewilderment creeps onto Norman's face. "Did you come to The Kee?"

"We came to The Kee," says Luccio.

"How come I didn't see you?"

"The question," says Luccio, shoving his forefinger up under Norman's chin, "is, How come we didn't see you?"

"I was there!" protests Norman, swatting Luccio's hand away.

"On *stage!*" says Luccio.

"What time?"

"Never mind what time!" says Luccio. He looks away as if to collect himself, and his voice drops to a bloodless calm. "We drove a hundred and twenty-five miles because you told us you were going to be playing with your band in Bala. We went all that way to support a friend, and when we got there we discovered that our friend obviously didn't feel the same way about us—that he'd bullshitted us, that he wasn't even in the band."

"Whaddaya mean not in the band?"

"You're not in the band!"

"Bets?" blurts Norman, throwing his open hand forward.

"I made my bet when I drove two hours to see you play," says Luccio, ramming a thick finger into Norman's shoulder.

"If I'm not in the band, how do you think I got these?" protests Norman, who thrusts out his hand, palm up, indicating the calluses that the guitar strings have made on his fingertips.

"You probably got them picking your ass," says Luccio without looking at them.

"You're fulla shit!"

"The problem," says Luccio "is that *you're* fulla shit! And I'd squeeze it outta you this minute, except I don't wanta spray it all over Angelo's truck. You're an equipment man, Norman, a roadie, and if you're smart, you'll get comfortable with that. Right now, just fuck off! Gimme a coffee, double double, and an Eat-More," he says to Angelo, who has been watching with ripening apprehension.

"You see these?" says Norman, turning to me as Luccio wanders off. He displays his calluses like a row of tiny medals. "Where did they come from if I don't play guitar?"

"Nobody's saying you don't play guitar," I tell him. I give him a slap of support on the shoulder and in a moment of raw awareness see him not as the cocky teenager we've gotten to know but as a pimple-faced child whose identity and self-esteem, however falsely he has shaped them, are being ripped away by thugs.

"Norman," I say to him in an attempt to redress the damage, "we asked the bass player if you were going to be playing, and . . . you know . . . What are we supposed to think?"

He looks at me out of some contemptuous corner of his shame and says, "Think whatever you want, Charlie. Fuck both of you!" He throws his chin out, orders a Coke, picks up the rake he has been using and strides off, plunking himself down by the trunk of a big black ash. By this time, Peter and the rest have gathered by the truck.

Luccio returns from the outhouse and says to no one in particular. "Have you heard that Norman's landed a job playing kazoo in the New York Philharmonic? See those little calluses on his lips."

In a flash, Norman is on his feet, rake in hand, moving at speed toward Luccio, who has turned his back. A chorus of shouted warnings comes too late, and the rake handle bounces with a *pong* off the back of Luccio's skull.

Luccio spins, apparently unfazed by the blow, and is on Norman like a grizzly, sending a boot into his backside with a thick *whap* that drives Norman chin-first into the grass. Luccio picks him up by the shirt and smacks him against a tree, in such a way that Norman's feet dangle several inches above the ground. "You skinny fuck," he says quietly. "I oughta bury you right here and now—without even digging a grave."

In an instant, Peter is behind him, attempting to pry him off. "Let him down!" he cries. "You're gonna hurt him!" Already, tears are cascading down Norman's cheeks, and, from Luccio's fists rammed up under his chin, his face has turned an alarming shade of red. A trickle of blood has appeared on Luccio's scalp, seeping downward onto his neck and collar. With Peter and Hogjaw, I try to pull him away, but he deflects us like so many minor insults. As Norman seems on the verge of passing out, I wedge my forearm up under Luccio's wrist, bring my mouth to within inches of his ear and scream at him to let go. He swings his face toward me and, as if emerging from a trance, releases his grip, allowing Norman to fall to the ground.

"Fuck you, you fucking fucker!" bawls Norman, tottering to his feet. But his rage brings no response.

Peter is immediately beside him, has him by the arm, fervently urging him to sit for a minute on the grass. But he won't. "Then go on up to the shop," Peter says quietly. "I wanta talk to you. I'll be there in a minute."

Looking mauled, not broken, and apparently as stubborn as ever, Norman shuffles across the lawn toward the road.

I follow Luccio out into the Garden of the Blessed Redeemer. "Did you know you're cut?" I ask as I come up behind him.

He walks a few steps and turns to me, eyes glazed and distant, face the colour of salmon flesh. "The question my friend is not what *I* know or don't know but whether *anybody* around here knows the difference between the mutant fucking horse thieves who control places like this and the zillions of pitiful doormats who don't even control their own arse lint?"

"No," I say, "that's not the question right now at all. Lemme see the back of your head."

"It's organization," he says softly. "And I'm not talking about the gawdam Teamsters or the cocksuckers union. They're only organized as long as it's profitable for the venal assholes who are *better* organized..."

"Did you hear what I said?" I ask more pointedly, having watched the blood spot on the back of his shirt expand until it's as big around as a saucer. But he pays no attention. He walks further into Blessed Redeemer, ranting, flinging his hands, jerking his head around with such violence that at one point a few drops of blood fly off into the air: "There they live on the crest of the gawdam hill," he protests, "while some weedy little fucker busts his ass forty hours a day, breaking his balls for some brain-damaged ape with a hard-on for a dollar—do you know what I can't stand?" he says, turning to me, pushing out his chin.

"Did you hear what I said?" I ask.

He glares at me, apparently taken aback at the impertinence of my interruption. "About what?" he demands, as he pops through the membrane, aiming his bulging eyes directly at mine.

"You're bleeding," I tell him.

"What are you talking about?"

"Touch the back of your head!"

He runs his fingers over his scalp, emitting a dog-like yelp at the sight of his blood-covered hand.

"Turn around," I tell him. "Lemme see." I part the sticky hair, laying bare a swelling as big as half a tennis ball and a gaping two-inch cut that it seems has penetrated to bone. I tear off my T-shirt, bunch it and order him to hold it against his head while I go for the car.

As we race toward the East General, he says, "Did Norman do this?"

"You deserved it," I tell him.

As we enter the emergency ward, he informs me that he has no medical insurance. I dig into my wallet and hand him my own card, which he examines, faintly befuddled, before shoving it into his pocket.

"Don't forget you're me," I tell him. "Ten Park Vista."

In the examining room, a pleasant middle-aged nurse grabs the flesh on the back of his neck, drives a two-inch hypodermic into it and pumps in the painkiller. With the patient mildly sedated, she washes the back of his head and shaves onto it an oblong bald spot, a fleshy purple matte for the ten neat stitches that, minutes later, a sprightly young female doctor in street clothes punches into his scalp. The impression created by the stitched wound is that of death lips with spiky black teeth, over which the nurse applies a flesh-coloured bandage as big as a baseball card.

As the pneumatic young physician examines Luccio's eyes and reflexes, I leave to move the car from its temporary parking spot by the emergency entrance. When I get back, Luccio, still naked from the waist up, and the doctor are standing by the door of the examining room in sober debate.

"Are you going to be with him for a while?" the doctor asks as I come within earshot.

"I wasn't counting on it," I tell her, "but I can be."

She says, "I suspect he's got a concussion, probably some short-term memory loss. I'd prefer if he'd stay here for a few hours, but if he won't, somebody should definitely be with him for a while."

"Why don't you stay here?" I ask him.

"Too much to do," he says.

"The main thing is to get off your feet when you get home," she says. "Take a day or two off."

Even before we leave the hospital, Luccio has initiated a low-grade muttering over the now-impaired prospects for his interview, which is scheduled for the day after tomorrow.

"What's more important, your interview or your life?" I ask him as we cross the parking lot.

"My interview," he says flatly.

We hit the 401 in the heart of rush hour and lurch across the top of the city, inhaling exhaust, rarely getting above twenty miles an hour. At the apartment, the blinds are closed, and the moist air smells faintly of toiletries and laundry soap—not so much of Lucy's absence as her departed presence. Newspapers and clothing are scattered across the living room, and unwashed dishes sit on almost every horizontal surface. I glance into her bedroom, where the only light comes from the fiery little numbers on the clock radio—6:22.

Luccio goes into the bathroom, picks up a hand mirror and aims it over his shoulder, so that he can see the back of his head in the mirror above the sink. "The only gawdam day in two years when I need to look real," he says, "and I look like fucking roadkill."

As he comes into the hall, he says, "Tell Peter I won't be in tomorrow."

"You tell him!"

He walks into the living room and opens the balcony door.

"How's the pain?" I ask him.

"Beautiful. Demerol."

"Do you want me to stay?"

"What for?"

"What if you hemorrhage, or something? You heard her."

"What are you gonna do, brain surgery? Get outta here."

As so often with Luccio, I am caught momentarily in a small private no-man's land, not quite sure whether to advance or retreat. In this case I advance—literally—around a puddle of newspapers and pizza boxes, and wish him well with his interview and hold out my hand to him. He shakes it and, in a rare moment of sincerity, thanks me for my help.

"You don't deserve it," I tell him.

"You're a true angel of light," he says.

"Let me know what happens," I tell him.

"I'll think about it."

I stand fidgeting in the doorway, looking not so much at Luccio as into the living room and across it out the window.

After a few seconds, he says, "What can I do for you?"

"Nothing," I shrug.

"What's going on?" he says.

"Are we gonna see you again at work?"

"That depends," he says, shaping his lips into an inscrutable smile.

"On what?" I ask.

"The unthinkable," he says. "Otherwise, on whether or not they're willing to mail a paycheque. As of this afternoon they owe me for eleven days. If they'll mail it I don't have to pick it up."

I tell him I could bring it to him.

"If they'll hand it over."

"You gonna phone me?"

"Do you want it in writing?"

I emerge from the doorway into the dark carpeted hallway, where the air seems suddenly devoid of oxygen.

"Good luck!" I call from the top of the stairwell.

But there is no response—just the quiet click of the apartment door behind me and the faint roar of the traffic from beyond the stairwell window.

PART two

Sixteen

THE MOST LIBERATED

LOCALITY ON EARTH

WHETHER OR not I saw Luccio again is a point of personal conjecture. I may have seen him from across the street one night in front of Basell's Restaurant at Gerrard and Yonge, or at a distance one afternoon loping across the Garden of Remembrance, perhaps with his last paycheque.

Whatever the case, he was gone from my days—and I missed him, even resented him for getting out. And yet from that point forward, perhaps more than before, the long hours on the mower, or by the coffins and stiffs as we lowered them into the earth, were defined by him, by his bittersweet absence, or more accurately (as with Lucy the previous day) by his departed presence.

The following morning just before eight o'clock, word went round that Norman had been fired for his daring battery of the previous afternoon. But when I spoke to Peter outside the shop, he denied it, claiming that Norman had been "suspended" for a couple of days to keep him out of Luccio's way, and that he had quit in umbrage over the injustice of this "protective" reprimand.

"And now gawdam Luccio's away anyway!" scoffed Peter, who looked at me with what I took to be skepticism but may have been nothing more than his chagrin over losing two employees with one swing of a rake handle. With Fred still off and with Peter ascended from the ranks of the working stiffs, the labour fórce was at an all-time low. To make matters worse, Denise Elizabeth Chartraw had been unable to start the previous day because of difficulties in liberating herself from her babysitting gig, and would not be in until Wednesday.

As for Luccio, I explained to Peter that he'd been hit hard enough to open a ten-stitch cut, and that he had been told to spend a couple of days in bed.

"He could gawdam phone me," said Peter, and he leaned into the window of his car and pulled out a clipboard that held the day's funeral orders. He flipped through them and said, "I want you to go with Hogjaw on the digger."

"Hogjaw's on the digger?"

"Somebody's gotta dig the fucking holes!"

The fact that that somebody was Hogjaw marked a passage indeed at Willowlawn, given that the last time Hogjaw had machine-dug a grave he'd carved up the neighbouring grave with such appalling brutality that Scotty had vowed he'd never mount the backhoe again.

"It's none of my business," I ventured, "but have you given any thought to hiring anybody besides the girl?"

"You working too hard?" said Peter, as if in nabbing Scotty's job he had inherited a measure of his sarcasm.

"Just a question."

He threw the clipboard into the car and said, "We're running an ad," and as he walked away, "Career opportunity—nowhere to go but down!"

Barely twenty minutes had passed when I spotted Norman himself strolling down the main road, looking as if he owned the institution. As if to snub the place once and for all, he was wearing his ceremonial Buffalo-bought "tux."

Above the growl of the backhoe, I explained to Hogjaw that I'd be back in a minute, trotted out to the road and called to Norman, who turned and waited, kicking at the edge of the lawn, as if attempting to toe a dime beneath a carpet. He had his hands stuffed in his back pockets, and it occurred to me that it was the first time since June that I'd seen him with seconds to kill and not fingering his imaginary guitar. "You're back!" I enthused as I came up to him, and asked him what had happened.

"Just to pick up my cheque," he said and, without missing a beat, he dropped his jaw and sounded a resonantly protracted burp.

"What happened?"

"Peter suspended me," he said, adding that he told Peter he'd quit if Peter didn't suspend Luccio, too. "And he didn't, so I did."

"He didn't do it as a punishment!" I said. "He did it to get you out of here, away from Luccio."

"I'm not afraid of Luccio!"

"You don't have to be—he's flat on his back. You nearly killed him."

"He nearly killed me!" said Norman, stretching the neck of his T-shirt, revealing a cluster of plum-coloured bruises.

"You're a lot better off than Luccio."

"Whaddaya mean?"

"He had a brain hemorrhage."

One of Norman's eyes fluttered. "You're puttin me on," he said.

"Do you think I'd joke about it? He went into a coma overnight. I visited him before I came to work."

"You're shittin me."

"I'm shittin ya," I said. "He's right over there. If he sees ya, you're dust."

Norman glanced over his shoulder.

I said, "I'm still shittin ya. He's at home. You gave him a con-cussion and ten stitches."

"Good," he said.

"Not for him it's not."

By this time, Norman had kicked up eighteen inches of lawn edging, a lumpy sod snake that he now caught on his toe and flipped lithely over his head. "What'd he say?" he asked without looking at me.

"About what?"

"About me!"

I said, "I imagine he's pretty pissed. He was already pissed, and you made it worse."

He kicked another chunk of sod, and said, "He was the ass-hole, not me!"

I attempted to explain to him that Luccio's behaviour was not strictly a response to what had happened in Bala, or even to being beaten on the back of the head. I considered a more thor-ough explanation, but the thought of it vanished as Norman's arm drifted out from his side, his hand formed a claw, and he proceeded into a soundless riff on his familiar fantasy Fender.

As I watched his rail-thin form recede up the road toward the shop, I felt a pang of regret at having seen the last of him—then of bemusement at seeing him saunter up to the snack truck at coffee break and announce disdainfully that he'd been rehired with a five-cent-an-hour raise.

"What'd you do for the nickel?" said Hogjaw, making an ugly little donut of his lips.

"What are ya gonna do when Luccio comes back?" chirped David.

"I'm going to express my deepest apologies," grinned Nor-man, using a phrase he had copped from Peter, who, he claimed, had taken him back on the condition that he extend "a heartfelt apology" to his departed nemesis.

"Apologies mean nothing to Luccio," said Hogjaw.

"Then I won't give him one," said Norman, who for a few seconds seemed to consider the plausibility of his response and, apparently happy with it, turned his attention to the handful of strawberry Twizzlers and the lime-flavoured Slurpee that were his mid-morning snack.

THE WORKFORCE got an added boost that afternoon when Fred showed up, clearly shaken by the state of the gardens. He was visibly stronger, but where once there had been flesh on his hands and forearms, there was now little but a layer of yellowed parchment. His eyes and mouth were the same spectral howl they had been at the funeral, and his voice was a brittle parody of its old self. More than anything, however, it was his bony skull that defined the new man—a startling Halloween jape, which if you glanced quickly at him seemed somehow to have migrated to the exterior of his face and scalp. Ever inventive, he had gathered an inch-deep tuck in the back of his shirt and had hand-stitched it, creating a kind of dorsal fin that angled across his backbone perhaps ten degrees off perpendicular. It was only as he left the shop pushing his implement cart that I noticed a similar gathering of fabric down the seat of his pants.

During the early afternoon I rode the sit-down mower, daydreaming as I rattled across the lawns, thinking occasionally about Luccio and how for me, in his seditious way, he had transformed this infested carpet of decomp and embalming compounds into what at times was the most liberated locality on earth. At one point I dozed off, awakening with a start as one of the mower blades caught a newly planted birch sapling, tearing off much of its bark and foliage. I got off and straightened the thing, feeling badly that I had ruined a twenty-dollar tree but cheerful that I wouldn't have to face Scotty over it.

Hungrier than usual at break, I ignored the snack truck and ran across the street to Hazel's Caribbean Hideaway, returning with the specialty of the house, a "Bongoburger" slithery with fried peppers and perhaps a week's ration of trans-homicidal fats. I sat briefly on the lawn with David and inquired about his grandfather, who he told me had spent most of the past week with David's parents and had significantly trimmed his daytime drinking. Never one to withhold even the most tawdry of tidbits, he allowed that Scotty was still pounding it after dark and that early one morning his mother had discovered him in the rec room staring pie-eyed at the television test pattern, an empty Cutty bottle on the coffee table in front of him. When I mentioned this to Peter, he told me that on a stormy morning last January, he and Hogjaw had arrived for work and had discovered the old man still at his desk from the previous day, soiled, passed out, sinking gradually into a hypothermic coma because the thermostat had been turned down to fifty degrees overnight. Unwilling to clean him up or even attempt to bring him round, Hogjaw had unbolted the bucket from a number-ten wheelbarrow and he and Peter had used it to cart Scotty down the stairs and then on home in his own car.

THE FOLLOWING morning, Denise Chartraw made her much-awaited debut, entering the charnel-yard in cut-off blue jeans and a sleeveless pop-top of such alluring flimsiness that, like the rest of the employees, I spent the better part of the morning in private consideration of the nifty blue bra, with contents, that was breathlessly visible beneath her little hippie blouse. At break, amidst the inevitable male chatter, Peter took mock affront to how readily we "fucked-up pigs" could be moved to ignore that there was invariably a sensitive being attached to even the most preposterous rib rockets, and of course also to the straps, cups and latches that, to his mind, were among the fashion industry's all-time great incentives to male fantasy.

It wasn't until nearly quitting time, as I cut the sod off one of the next day's graves, that I had an opportunity to speak to Denise Elizabeth, who came quietly through the nearby thicket and said without preamble, "How deep do you dig those things?"

"Just deep enough to be legal," I told her and explained that, by law, a body had to have at least four feet of soil above it—but not six as most people believed. (There were in fact corpses at Willowlawn covered by little more than three feet of soil, in particular the top-dwellers in thrift plots or double-deckers—this to say nothing of bones that had been tossed in the Quarry and were now covered, if at all, by an inch or two of rotted irises or chrysanthemums.)

In the course of a twenty-minute conversation, Denise confided to me, among other things, that she had been playing the cello for nine of her seventeen years, that she had three sisters, all older, and that a few weeks hence she would be entering the University of Toronto to study anthropology and French literature. I told her I myself had been at U of T for two years—University College—and suggested I take her down there some evening and show her around.

She said, "Do you own the red car?"

"I do," I said, to which she responded that she loved sports cars, adding that her dad, a Belgian metallurgist, had once owned an Austin Healey, had crashed it, had broken his back doing so, and, as the family grew, had settled unhappily for American sedans and, eventually, station wagons. She confided that her dad, a lifelong Gitanes smoker, was battling lung cancer, final stages, and that money was tight at home, which had precipitated her application to the cemetery. She stared at the naked earth, where I had cut the sod and said, "It's just so eerie think-ing about being down there."

As we walked toward the shop, she volunteered that what she wanted most for her dad at this stage was that he'd "just find some peace"—an end to the non-stop coughing that for him, as well as the rest of the family, had become an insufferable and constant burden. When we were about to part ways, she said, "When did you think we might go down to the university?"

I said, "Whenever you like," to which she replied that she'd be available any night next week—which by chance coincided with opportunities in my own rather lightly booked social agenda.

I DID not hear from Luccio that evening or the next, and hesi-tated to call on the chance that things had gone badly. I consid-ered, too, of course, that things had gone well, and that he might already be installed in a studded leather chair, with perhaps a studded leather secretary, and had in short order relegated me to a distant corner of his eminently forgettable past. It was one of Luccio's sustaining assets that, at least temporarily, he could camouflage himself into any number of landscapes or circum-stances—including, I was sure, the corporate or institutional monkey cage. I was just as sure that his true inclinations would eventually put him back in touch with me.

Seventeen

AS DEEPLY ADRIFT AS EVER

THE FOLLOWING day, Scotty showed up mid-morning and spent an hour or two tottering around the grounds, grumbling about the decline of the place in his absence. He returned the following morning, setting a pattern of daily appearances that would continue into early September. According to David, he was at home again, where the family's chief concern was that he was living on Marmite and cocktail wieners—and of course two thousand calories a day in liquid brain retardant. He had resumed his drinking to a point where the family had felt it necessary to confiscate the keys to his car.

Word was that Peter would keep his management position only until Scotty was "ready to resume his responsibilities." Al had been around and had apparently put Peter on notice. However, as each day passed, it became clearer that Scotty would not be ready to resume in this life or the next. By the time his taxi arrived in the early afternoon to pick him up, he invariably needed all the ingenuity he could muster to accomplish the trip from the shop or statuary garden to the parking lot.

One morning as I cut through the Garden of the Apostles of the Living Christ, a favourite of Scotty's, I found him seated on a bench in the statuary enclave. His fedora had slipped onto his forehead, obscuring his eyes.

"Scotty?" I said, moving to within a step of him, bending to peer under his hat brim. "You okay?"

"Fine!" he blurted. "Whatime is it?"

"Eleven-thirty."

"Si'down, si'down," he said.

I told him I should probably keep moving—was supposed to be over in Redeemer doing sinkers.

He asked about the new boy, and I told him the boy was a girl, and that she'd just started.

"Just started!" he barked. "The gawdam summer's over!"

I explained that we were short of workers what with Fred sick and Peter filling in as manager. "Plus," I said, "Luccio's been away." I mentioned Monday's fracas, at which he raised his hat brim, aimed his cataracts in my direction and whispered, "You don't say."

When I told him Denise's dad was dying and that she needed the job, he responded with apparent sobriety that I should let the boys in the office know—that with his "son" working here he might qualify for a plot discount.

For several seconds, he stared into the shrubbery, then focused himself and told me he was on his way over to Mrs. MacKinnon's grave. He said, "I want you to come out there and clean it up. Every gawdam flower on it's dead."

It occurred to me to argue that the flowers had been dead when they were placed on the grave, and that what they were now was wilted. But instead I repeated that we were short of workers and told him that before I did anything I should check with Peter.

"I'll tell him myself," he said. "Come on!" And he stood up and took a few wonky steps across the flagstones.

We had walked perhaps twenty-five yards in the direction of the grave, when he stopped on the footpath and did a ninety-degree turn in much the way a tin soldier might accomplish the manoeuvre. "I've bought two lilac bushes," he announced. "Double French hybrids, Maréchal de Bassompierre. I'm gonna plant one of them by Mrs. MacKinnon's grave as a memorial to her and put the other in Last Supper as a tribute to Fred."

I told him I liked his choice, and he said it was the least he could do, adding that Fred was "the best gawdam worker" the cemetery ever had. "Don't tell him," he said. "We'll have a ceremony. I shoulda got him a gawdam arm in 1945."

I said, "At least he'll have a lilac bush," but the joke went unacknowledged as Scotty attempted another couple of steps and tottered slightly, spreading his feet for balance. "You go on ahead," he said. "You know where the grave is. I'll catch up," and he turned uncertainly toward the road.

LATE THE following afternoon, momentarily lucid, Scotty came upon me in the shop and urged me up to the office that he now shared with Peter. Rather than create friction, Peter had been working out of his car, where he kept the plot maps and grave orders, as well as the daily assignment sheet. The office was in its usual state of barely sublimated chaos. An array of boxes and loose files had appeared since I sat in the place the previous Saturday and was scattered willy-nilly across the desk, the floor, the windowsills. Whereas once there had been at least standing room, there was now a sense that if you were going to get past the door you'd best scramble up and over and settle somewhere on top. The only visible sign of the evolving shift in management was an ostentatious new wall calendar from the Trull Funeral Home, showing an artless seascape and promising "compassion," "understanding" and "city-wide limo service."

As always, such considerations came with "easy terms" and at "affordable costs," phrases that, in the arcane vocabulary of the death trade, tended to translate as "convoluted financial traps" and "excessive hidden charges."

Scotty's copy of *Midnight* lay on the desk, its front page emblazoned with the news that the Pope had absolved the recently dead Jayne Mansfield of her sins and that her voluptuous ghost, secretly resurrected, was "living the screen-star lifestyle" in the decadent recesses of the Vatican.

Meanwhile, I puddle-stepped across the floor and sat on a stack of old BalsamBlast boxes. The air smelled of liniment, and the voice of Gordon Sinclair quacked from the radio. "Why," he demanded, "would anyone need airplanes as big as The Concorde and the 747," both of which had recently gone into transatlantic service, carrying as many as six hundred passengers. Scotty reached into his desk and withdrew a fifth of Cutty and two scummy glasses. He poured each of us three fingers, inhaled his own and poured another.

I fiddled with mine untouched, and for the better part of the next twenty minutes was a one-man audience for a rambling reminiscence on Scotty's early years in the land of no tomorrows. He explained without compunction that through much of the Depression, and into the war, he and the head gravedigger had routinely opened coffins after the mourners had gone and had pocketed dentures of the sort that, in the days before fluoridated water and high-tech dentistry, nearly everybody who'd survived middle age wore as a matter of course. By Scotty's accounting, every dozen sets he and his buddy collected brought them ten dollars from a man he described as "a brrrutal fucking Cherry Street junk merrrchant"—a man who, for modest profit, removed the acrylic teeth from the "gums" and jobbed them to supply-deprived denture makers.

"Me 'n' five fucking Irishmen on the graves," he said "Pick and shovel. Worked from seven in the morning till six at night, with half an hour for lunch. If ya weren't finished at quitting time, ya worked till ya were!"

Scotty recalled Catherine coming into the cemetery on summer nights, bringing him his supper and a fresh thermos of tea. "And two little ones trailing behind her."

He poured himself another shot, leaned toward me and said, "We staggered outta here. Never even took a coffee break— never *heard* of a coffee break. We'd'a been fired on the spot for sitting fifteen minutes on our asses on the grass! No union. No pension. No workman's comp. No hospital or unemployment insurance. And I'll tell ya something," he said. "We had no gawdam complainers."

The shortage of labour toward the end of the war brought with it a promotion to foreman, in charge of a workforce that, by Scotty's estimation, included "every fuck-up and layabout" that the war had no use for and the municipality felt should be working for their food vouchers. He worked his khakis out of his crack and explained that he, too, would have been overseas except that his feet were "as flat as gawdam canoe paddles." He made a half-hearted attempt to raise his shoe into view, as though the severity of the prolapse might be visible through a half-inch of cobbling. "We had so many gawdam Victory Gardens in Blessed Virgin," he said, "we could'a fed half the city on squash and beans." A little burn of Scotch escaped his lower lip, prompting him to pull a revolting-looking handkerchief from his pants pocket and swipe first at his chin and then at the drop of clear mucus that had settled on the septum of his nose. After a fumbled attempt to reinstall the hanky, he looked at it fondly and tossed it on the floor. He said, "All that of course was before this current gawdam management came along. Don't know shit from shinola." He stared out the window into the foliage of the nearby hardwoods, then at his hands and said, "I gave my life to this fucking place, and all they've wanted for ten years is to get rid of me." A grin twisted his face. "But they can't," he said, his voice rising suddenly into a self-ingratiating falsetto. "I know way too gawdam much!"

He reached into the drawer, poured another ounce of Cutty, applied it unsteadily and said, "I know every horseshit crime and illegality that's gone on here in thirty-eight years." He said he had seen bodies buried out along the fences without even a death certificate, some of them carved up like turkeys. "Couldn't even tell whether they were men or women. Seen more than one with a bullet in his head."

He tossed back another shot and said, "The only gawdam way they're gonna get me outta here is when I'm good and ready to go. Either that or in a box. And even then they won't get ridda me, cause I'll be right out there in Redeemer by the lilacs—I'll control the place from underground! I'll organize the gawdam stiffs!"

He dragged the back of his hand across his mouth and for a few seconds seemed to be asleep. When he opened his eyes, he stared onto his desk, then across it into the mystic fetches somewhere beyond my shoulder. "If you want it," he said, rolling his eyes, "I can give ya full-time gawdam employment."

I sat contemplating the farce that would be permanent work at Willowlawn, doubting that Scotty had the power to hire me even if I did want it. I said, "I'm not sure I wanta go full time."

"Whadelsh ya gonna do?" he demanded, my response to which had barely begun to formulate itself when he screamed, "Stop!" and held up his hand. "I know what you're gonna say! You're gonna tell me you're gonna teach! Am I right?"

As I opened my mouth to say I was thinking more of travel, he howled, "Anybody can teach! All ya need is a shaving kit and a gawdam alarm clock! Check your brains at the gawdam door!" He straightened in his chair and said, "Young fella like you could run this place some day! Doesn't even need running! First thing I do when I get to my office in the morning is read the gawdam newspaper. Then I have a nap. Then I go for lunch. Then I have another nap. And of course I have this," he said, flicking a finger in the direction of the near-empty Cutty Sark bottle. "Ya stay with it," he said, "and one day you can do anything you want around here."

He reached for the bottle, poured the last dizzying drops into his glass and tossed them back. Then he attempted to stand. But as he straightened his legs one of his knees gave way, and he flopped back onto his chair, the shock of it causing his jaw to fall slack and a kind of tremor to freeze the deep-scored flesh around his eyes.

As I dialled a cab, his head hit the desk, flipping his fedora onto the papers in front of him, brim up. I completed the call, got up and shaped a pillow out of a windbreaker that hung on the coat tree with several items of old rainwear. I slipped it beneath his skull, sat down and, as I waited for the cab, read an *Enquirer* story headlined "Movie legend Elizabeth Taylor gives slip to zipper magnate."

Then with all but scientific curiosity, I leaned forward and studied Scotty's face—its loose folds and poorly shaved whiskers, its million snapped capillaries. In a more just, perhaps more literary, world, I might have hoped that he'd just die there, expire painlessly where he was. But things being what they were—the hour past quitting time, his fortitude legendary—it was all I could do for the moment to hope that his rectal muscles would hold and that he wouldn't soil his pants or vomit onto himself before the cab arrived to trundle him away.

A few minutes later, I led the driver up into the office. Scotty by this time was lolling over the arm of his chair, threatening to capsize the thing. We looked at him in much the way a couple of engineers might scrutinize a delicate disposal operation. I said, "How do you want to do it?"

"I don't," he said, and he turned and descended the stairs, leaving me with an urge to heave the cremation casket on the desk at the back of his capped head.

"Fuck you!" I said as he disappeared from sight.

A second later he was back, his pear-shaped silhouette filling the bottom of the stairwell. "Did you say something?"

"I was talking to him."

"That's what I thought," he said, and again he disappeared.

I turned to Scotty, who was now snoring, his mouth forming a bluish spittoon that I was tempted to stuff with newspaper. "Fuck you, too," I said, and I clomped down the stairs and out through the shop. It was nearly 5:30, and as I reached the parking lot it occurred to me that, except for Scotty, I was the last employee on the premises. I stood for a few seconds, weighing the consequences of abandoning him—saw myself arriving for work in the morning and being told that he had suffocated in vomit, or died of alcoholic shock (although the latter was unlikely, given the massive consumption that he had been accustomed to for thirty years). I considered phoning his daughter, David's mother. Then I remembered that, even after four months of working with David, I didn't know his last name— had heard it but had forgotten.

I tramped back upstairs, righted Scotty in his chair and hollered at him to WAKE THE HELL UP. His eyes fluttered, and he muttered for a second or two before lapsing back into unconsciousness. With the trepidation of a rookie proctologist, I reached into his pants pocket, extracted his wallet, removed his driver's licence and read his address, on a street I knew, just south of Woodlawn Road. In his other pocket I found keys, one of which seemed to be a house key.

I stared at him for a moment, stepped behind him, and, reaching under his arms, raised him out of his chair. He was lighter than I had expected but not so light that I felt confident about picking him up and attempting to carry him down the stairs. Instead, I dragged him on his heels, bumping over and around boxes, then swung him around and, feet first, eased him over the precipice. Halfway down and beginning to lose my grip, I lowered him onto his backside and slid him to the bottom.

Leaving him sprawled on the landing, I punched my time card and left the shop. The afternoon had turned cool, and a sharp band of iron-grey cloud had appeared in the north— a first hint of autumn. As I walked toward my car, a city bus, a CNE Special, pulled up opposite the main gates, and half a dozen Exhibition-goers got off, one of them carrying three or four stuffed animals, another a massive pink teddy bear. Such creatures had an unlikely and poignant presence at the cemetery, where they were occasionally placed in the open graves of children, on top of the coffins, sometimes half a dozen of them, or set on graves, later, to commemorate birthdays. I put the car-top down, drove into the shop and horsed Scotty into the passenger seat. But before I could circle the car and get behind the wheel, he jackknifed in slow motion, his forehead thudding into the dash. I hoisted him upright and, holding him with one arm, removed his tartan necktie, looped it around his chest and knotted it behind the seat.

Fifteen minutes later, I had him laid out on his own comfy Sleep Queen—belt loosened, shirt and shoes off. I stood looking at him, my sense of accomplishment at getting him there tempered only by a notion that I should probably try to get him to the toilet. But I didn't feel like it. Instead, I pulled the blind, left the room and took a quick tour of the small brick bungalow where Scotty and Catherine had spent the better part of their lives. My curiosity fell somewhere between that of an anthropologist and a peeping Tom as I poked through rooms crammed with tweedy, nondescript furniture, Victorian carpeting, yellowed doilies, feckless framed prints. On the kitchen table, where presumably pork chops and roast chickens once sizzled, a plastic tray bore a banquet of potions and pills. A too-small back window looked out on a too-small backyard. The only thing in the house that seemed disproportionately large was a king-sized box of Kellogg's All-Bran, the cathartic brown regulator of the dammed. Everywhere, the long months of Catherine MacKinnon's illness hung in the air, a palpable accretion of medicines, antiseptics and body effluents. The smell was strongest in the living room, where I gathered she had spent her last days, on a dusty couch, in the company of soap opera lizards and game show hosts.

Before leaving, I glanced in at Scotty and was surprised to find him sitting like Lazarus, upright, wired, decidedly back from the dead. He stared at me, apparently fully conscious, and quacked, "Ya stay at the graveyard three years, and you get your choice of a free burial plot. Any garden ya want," and he collapsed back on the mattress.

I turned on the light, walked to the edge of the bed and found him as deeply adrift as ever.

eighteen

HOUSEKEEPING AND

HUMAN DISPOSITION

TWO MORNINGS later, Peter poked his head into the change shed as I pulled on my work clothes and asked if I knew anything about Luccio.

"No," I said, "do you?"

"He phoned Friday—that's the last I heard from him."

"Have you phoned him?" I said.

"Can't get an answer."

That evening, I phoned the apartment but, like Peter, got no response. Five days had passed since I'd seen Luccio, and the following day at coffee break I phoned Imperial Oil and asked for him in Financial Planning. A ritually pleasant woman informed me that no one by that name worked in the department.

"He'd be new," I said.

"I know everyone here. I'm sorry."

I asked at the switchboard if he was *anywhere* in the company and was transferred to yet another receptionist and on to the assistant personnel manager, a weary-sounding careerist, who treated me with respectful forbearance.

"He's a friend," I explained, and was told that, yes, there had been an interview, but that Mr. Pucci would not be joining Imperial—at least not at "this point in time."

On a flyer, I phoned the North York General Hospital, but he wasn't there.

ON THE Wednesday before Labour Day, Peter drove the front-end loader into the maintenance shop, parked it with its bucket at the bottom of the stairs, and asked me to get Denise and join him in Scotty's office. For the better part of the day, Denise and I sorted four decades of accumulated junk, shouldering load after load of mildewed refuse down the stairs. Out it all went—plant poisons, piss pots, prostheses, periodicals, seed and supply catalogues, work clothes dating to the Depression.

"Does Scotty know we're doing this?" I asked at break, to which Peter responded that he'd find out soon enough.

"Does he still have a job?" I said.

"He's our Alcoholic Emeritus," said Peter without breaking a smile. "His job when he shows up is to drink himself unconscious. And your job," he added, "is to stay the fuck out of his way—leave him alone. When you do what you did the other day, all you're doing is preventing people who have the power to get him out of here from seeing what's going on."

I told Peter that I hadn't wanted him to die at his desk.

"It's not your problem where he dies. And by the way, what's going on with Luccio?"

"Whaddaya mean 'going on'?"

"Don't fuck with me," he snapped. "I've got enough on my plate right now. You're his friend—where is he?"

I crossed my heart and told him I didn't have a clue.

"Is he coming back?" said Peter.

"Isn't he fired?"

"He has to *be* here to get fired! And if he were here, I'd pro-mote him, not fire him. I need him on the gawdam backhoe with Hogjaw."

Peter implored me to have Luccio call him. "Tell him Al's authorized me to raise everybody's pay."

"How much?" I demanded.

"For you, twenty-five cents."

"How much for Luccio?"

"A dollar," he said without looking at me.

"You think he's four times more valuable than I am?"

"I think he's ten times more valuable than you are. It's just that to pay him that much, I'd have to fire you!"

AMONG SCOTTY'S treasures were three or four hundred yel-lowed Christmas cards, mostly from funeral homes, a carton of business correspondence dating from the Second World War, and a scrapbook of press clippings on the multifarious intrigues of the death industry. I opened the scrapbook to a story on mob-owned funeral homes in Buffalo, in particular those of the Magaddino Family, which had made a specialty of the "two-tiered" coffin, the top tier of which carried a "viewable" corpse, the hidden understorey a victim whose fate, the clipping said, "was to go from the anonymity of the mob-owned mortuary to the anonymity of the mob-controlled cemetery."

A quite recent clipping showed a coroner's photo of the actress Sharon Tate, as well as one of the embalmed Marilyn Monroe. The caption below claimed that the latter's once-expansive frontage had been rendered so tattered and puny by autopsy procedures that the wife of the attending mortician had, as a consideration to her fans, lumped up a few dozen tissues and stuffed them into her bra.

Away it all went into garbage bins that, at quitting time,

Denise and I dragged into the administration wing, along with boxes of the more lumpish detritus that Scotty had scrounged over the decades and that I was reluctant to jettison as garbage: crucifixes, belt buckles, eyeglasses, vases. Scotty's new office was an airless junior-level cubicle, without privacy or windows, lit by his antique gooseneck and a pair of fluorescent tubes.

If there was a decisive stroke in the transition of authority to Peter, it occurred the following afternoon when, without consulting Scotty—without even informing him—Peter hired two more employees to plug a manpower shortage that would peak a few days hence when Norman and David returned to school.

On the same day, Peter was officially named operations manager and Hogjaw head gravedigger.

At quitting time that afternoon, as if to put the capstone on his ascendance, Peter backed the largest wagon on the premises, an old double-wheeler, into the shop, closed the shop doors and, using a thirty-two-ounce peening hammer, smashed the lock off the sub-basement room that had been Scotty's long-time bottle repository. Peter, Hogjaw and I entered the place in much the way William Flinders Petrie and his accomplices must have entered the Great Pyramid of Giza—self-appointed plunderers, wary of spiders and spectres. However, with the light on and the shadows routed, the surprises were less about spectres than about the pettiness of housekeeping and human disposition, the rituals of drunkenness and age. There it all was, the sad green reliquary in its sad brown light, shelf upon shelf of dusty bottles, stacked three deep, each with its top on, each with its familiar yellow label. The last desolate intrigue was that many of the bottles, perhaps hundreds, had never been fully drained and contained perhaps a tablespoon of mysteriously unspent fuel. Using a pair of steep-sided wheelbarrows, we rolled what must have been two thousand bottles up a foot-wide plank onto the wagon, then out to the Quarry under a khaki-coloured tarpaulin. And there, using shovels, we pushed the mountain of vessels into the depths, thirty, forty at a time, each a day in the life, the first of them landing softly in the compost, the rest clinking and smashing, some exploding with a pop, amidst the bottles and decomp and spent flowers.

THE NEXT day—Norman's last on the job before returning to school—he and I spent eight dusty hours removing shelves from the one-time bottle repository, scraping mould from the walls, then hosing them down in preparation for a coat of whitewash, all of it a precursor to the room's cheery new role as a storeroom for the implements of the grave.

A few minutes before quitting time, I said to Norman, "I guess that's about it for the summer!"

"I guess so," he shrugged.

I told him I was going to miss him, and he said, "I *am* in the band, ya know."

I said, "I know that."

He said, "What happened to Luccio?"

"I don't know," I said.

"Does he still wanta kill me?"

"I don't know."

"He still your friend?"

"I don't know."

At five o'clock I shook hands with Norman and David, both of whom bid me and the others a perfunctory goodbye and left the change shed, glad to be on their way.

However, as I left the shed a few minutes later, David was still in the parking lot, fiddling with the carburetor on his bike. I took the opportunity to ask him about Scotty, who I had not seen since the day I had driven him home. As far as David knew, his grandfather had no idea that Peter had been appointed foreman, or that his office had been cleaned out, or that he had been moved into the administrative part of the building. Al, he believed, had explained to Scotty that he should come back when he was rested and ready, not a moment sooner, and that there would always be a place for him at Willowlawn (*perhaps even above ground,* seemed to be the unspoken subtext of this fatuous cajolery).

"Is he coming back?" I said.

"Not if my mother has anything to do with it."

"And does she?" I said, and he told me that a couple of days earlier she had taken Scotty a meal and had found it the next day, untouched, in the bathroom, where she also discovered a half case of Cutty in the towel cupboard. When she had questioned Scotty about a bruise on his face, he admitted that he had slipped on the floor tiles, had injured not just his face but his knee, and had spent the better part of twelve hours sacked out on the bath mat, comforted only by the green-bottled alleviation that the Good Shepherd himself had placed in the john in anticipation of whatever might afflict Scotty, and wherever on earth it might afflict him.

I told David we had cleaned out the bottle room, and he said, "What bottle room?" And a few seconds later, he was on his way out of the cemetery, the hundred-and-forty-decibel wail of his little blue Kawasaki echoing among the gravestones.

THE FOLLOWING evening, just past dinner hour, I picked up Denise at the Chartraw family bungalow in Don Mills, and we breezed down the Don Valley Parkway into the shadow of the Bloor Street Viaduct, then west along Bloor toward the university. The Viaduct was embedded in my consciousness at the age of thirteen when, as my dad and I crossed it one day in the car, he told me that after returning from the war he had been wired and confused to the point where, as he walked home from university one night, he had stood for half an hour on the Viaduct, a hundred feet above the valley floor, weighing whether or not to end his life by jumping. What had saved him, he said, was that in the depths of his emptiness he had started to pray—had in fact prayed his way out of his predicament, so that when he walked off the bridge an hour later it was with a new sense of purpose and clarity.

I told Denise this, and as we were waiting at the light at Yonge, she looked at me, and said, "Do *you* pray?"

"Do you?" I said.

"All the time," she said.

I asked what she prayed for, and she said without hesitation, "For money, of course!" and she laughed and said that these days she prayed for her dad. "And for myself," she said. "I pray that I'll be there for him. And you?"

"When I feel like it," I said, to which she responded that I didn't sound very certain.

"I'm not."

"So why do you do it?"

"Just in case."

For an hour or more we walked around the university, then up through Queen's Park, and she told me she wouldn't even be going to U of T if it hadn't been for a five-hundred-dollar scholarship from her high school, Malvern Collegiate. "The problem," she said was that she'd "rather be studying theatre than anthropology."

As we walked back along Hoskin, I told her about Luccio, about his brashness and stubbornness and the fact that a short story he had written at the cemetery was about to be published. I told her how he had brightened my summer and had disappeared and how I missed him.

I thought about taking her hand, but didn't do it.

However, as we drove out Danforth Avenue, she reached over with both hands and briefly held my upper arm. As we crossed Woodbine, she said in a playfully conspiratorial voice, "Have you ever seen the cemetery at night?"

In fact I had—had gone back one night just after dusk to get my wallet, which I had left in the change shack, and had been surprised at how the darkness, rather than closing the world in and shutting it down, seemed to bring it alive, as in old vampire movies where men and women with long canines and bad Austrian accents stalked cemeteries in which the graves were laid open to the night.

"I haven't," I lied, and she said, "It's a full moon." And five minutes later we turned in the front gate, and I switched off the lights and drove slowly up the main road into the Garden of the Apostles of the Living Christ.

We walked out across the lawn, dodging headstones, and in the Garden of the Last Supper stopped at a mildewed sarcophagus that to my mind had always smelled faintly of Vicks Vapo-Rub, or perhaps embalming compounds, and leaned against it and began to neck. She was wearing blue jeans and a cotton top, and eventually I slid my hands up onto the soft skin of her back, then down into the band of her jeans, and held her against me. We returned to the car and got a blanket and went out into Blessed Redeemer and lay down among the willow trees in the darkness. A minute later she sat up, unhooked her bra and lay down again, more visible now that the clouds had sailed free of the full moon, which threw a silvery wash across the headstones and lawn and onto the cool white skin of her shoulders and breasts.

AN HOUR later, as we beetled up the Parkway into Don Mills, I reached over and took her hand, and she said without looking at me, "There's something I haven't told you, something I *should* have told you—I know I should have told you."

I looked over, and she looked away and withdrew her hand.

"Well, what is it?" I said.

"I have a boyfriend!"

I said, "At this rate, you're not gonna have one for long."

She said, "I've never thought of myself as a cheater," to which I explained that doing it in a cemetery didn't actually count as cheating, that there was an exemption for girls who took their clothes off on consecrated ground—"sort of a religious thing," I said, and she laughed and said, "I guess you can't get pregnant then."

"No, you can," I said. "Immaculate conception."

"Don't flatter yourself," she said, adding that if I ever told anybody at the cemetery—anybody, period—she'd never speak to me again. "And I mean that," she said.

All of which was more or less academic, in that she didn't speak to me the next day anyway, in fact wouldn't look at me, I suspect out of self-recrimination. At lunch hour two days later, she approached me in the shop and, still without looking me in the eye, apologized for what she referred to as her "behaviour."

I told her she had no reason to apologize, and she said, "I told Tim—well, I didn't tell him everything. And he told me to tell you I don't want to go out with you and that I'm sorry for doing what I did."

"And *are* you sorry?"

"Not particularly."

I asked her why she'd told him, and she said she "felt badly," and I told her I believed the only thing either of us had to feel badly about was that, the way things were going, we wouldn't have the chance to do what we did again—"certainly not if we have to ask your boyfriend."

"Maybe some day we won't," she said, and she walked purposefully out of the shop in the direction of the change shack, where the resident bone polishers had recently assigned her a locker and granted her changing rights.

OVER THE next few days, I made a passing attempt to get to know the new employees, one of whom, Sebastian, was an ex–elementary school teacher and, to my mind at least, a bona fide weirdo. During his second morning on the job, I laid out a grave with him, under Hogjaw's mulish eye. In the course of two hours, I asked him perhaps half a dozen questions about himself and got nothing but paranoid questions in response: Are you married? Are *you* married? Where ya from? Where are *you* from?

As we tidied up after the burial, he said out of the blue, "So what the fuck kinda place is this, anyway?"

I asked what he meant, feeling oddly defensive about a place I couldn't stand but to which I had more or less committed a summer of my life. "It's a burial ground," I said.

"Oh, it's a *burial ground*," he said. "I assume that's something like a graveyard. What I mean is, are they all like this?"

I told him I didn't follow, and he looked at me and said, "Run by DPS. Everywhere ya look around here there's another wetback."

Moved briefly to silence, then to indignation, I asked if it was true that he'd been a teacher.

"Nunna your business," he said, at which point I threw my broom in the wheelbarrow and headed for the shop.

THE OTHER new arrival, Dwayne, was equally unforthcoming, more out of shyness I gathered than bigotry. One day at break, as four or five of us sprawled on the lawn, he said, "I used to wonder what kinda people worked in graveyards. Now I know."

Amid a round of smirks and snickers, Peter said, "What kind?"

"Regular guys," he brightened. "As regular as any place I ever worked."

Before I could give voice to the thought that I had never met anyone at Willowlawn who I would describe as "a regular guy,"

Hogjaw blustered, "Where on God's fucking earth did you work that makes these guys look normal?"

Dwayne responded quite cheerfully that, among other jobs, he had been a garbage collector and an "electrocutionist" in a slaughterhouse—and, most recently, a janitor and lay preacher in a Pentecostal church.

"A priest?!" cried Sebastian.

"Preacher," grinned Dwayne, volunteering that for five years he had also been "a skid-row alky" and that the core of his message—the "secret of his ministry," as he put it—had invariably been to tell his congregation how bad it was among the back-alley rubbies and heroin addicts and, by contrast, how good it was to come into the "gracious saving power of the Lord Jesus Christ... *And you can come, too,*" he said sarcastically, holding his hands out, palms up, to an imaginary congregation. *"Come now, my friends ... Get up out of your seats and walk down the aisle ... Come to the Lord ... Christ is calling ..."*

He added that in his capacity as a preacher he had twice conducted funerals and burial services—once for an old man who had died nameless on the street, once for a young woman whose "entire frigging face," as he put it, had been erased, point-blank, by a shotgun.

"How did you know what to say?" asked Denise, to which he replied that he had taken it all "from a book" but that, in the young woman's case, amidst grieving relatives, he had broken down during the reading of the Twenty-third Psalm. "I got to the part about *goodness and mercy shall follow me all the days,* and I blew like a boiler—just gawdam wailed. I never did another one."

Dwayne admitted that he had been banned from the church several months ago for "going to bed" with one of the women in the choir—a Pentecostal no-no to which the woman had confessed in front of the church's aptly named "lay panel."

The fact that, after a week, I was still having trouble remembering the newcomers' names was more than a passing reflection of my broadening apathy toward anything and everything about the cemetery.

Mostly, I guess, I missed Luccio. On and off for ten days after his departure, I tried unsuccessfully to reach him by phone. Then one night, late, at home, I got a surprise call from Lucy, who was at the apartment, where she had apparently not been for several days. Luccio, she told me, was in Buffalo. He'd gone to Pittsburgh to meet with one of the professors who had adjudicated his dissertation. There had been a chance that a part-time teaching job would come of it. But it hadn't materialized, and wouldn't perhaps until Christmas, and now Canadian Immigration was refusing to allow him back into the country on his lapsed visa.

For the time being, she said, he was staying in a hostel of some sort. She said she wanted to get "some money and things" to him, and that if I wanted to do her and Luccio "a huge favour..."

After a few seconds, I said, "Well, what is it?" to which she responded in her most seductively girly voice that Luccio had felt that *maybe*—"just *maybe*"—I'd consider driving to Buffalo with her to take him what he needed to get his visa sorted out.

Juiced by the prospect of seeing Luccio, and equally by the thought of three or four hours in the car with Lucy, I said, "Of course!" And on the Sunday of the Labour Day weekend, at 8 A.M., I picked her up at her apartment in North York. She was wearing strappy sandals and a little floral miniskirt which, on the leather bucket seat, rode so far up her thighs as to be no skirt at all. She had packed a lunch basket and a small moss-coloured suitcase for Luccio, which fitted in the well behind the seats.

As we beat it along the Queen Elizabeth Way, we yattered enthusiastically about books, about music, about North

American taste in movies. In an Italian restaurant outside St. Catharines, she offered up a lavish assessment of the films of her countryman, Federico Fellini—*La Dolce Vita* was her favourite. The American film industry, she ventured, would never produce a work of art to match it. Fellini, she said, "understood fantasy, understood longing," and she proceeded to tell me that to understand the latter "without needing to resolve it" was, as she put it, to know "something meaningful about what it is to evolve as a human being."

I told her I'd never thought of it that way, and she said, "Of course you haven't, you're nineteen years old; you still think every longing has to be satisfied." She said the other thing Fellini understood was that the great themes of history—the "dialectical themes" as she put it—were not economic, as we had learned in first-year philosophy class, but were conceptual, were moral—were in fact injustice and survival.

At U.S. Customs, a middle-aged border guard stared shamelessly at her thighs and waved us on into Buffalo. We drove through a seedy section of the city and, with the help of a map, located the downtown flophouse where Luccio had apparently been holed up for several days. The concierge, a bulky young black man, sat as joyless as hemorrhoids in a kind of chain-link cage, poking the last bits of a Burger King Whopper into his mouth.

Lucy said, "I believe my brother's staying here."

"What's his name?"

"Luccio," she said, at which point the young man turned to the mail rack, turned back and said, "Yer too late—he's gone. What's yer name?"

She told him, and he took an envelope from his desk, showing her a name that had been scrawled across it in ballpoint. "Zat you?"

"Yes," she said.

"Yer brother ast me t' give it to ya."

She took it from him, thanked him, and as we stepped from the building launched a pleading, almost tearful, apology—*how could he have stranded us like this? How could he have not let her know?*

"Read it!" I urged her, and she tore open the envelope and removed a single leaf of typewriter paper covered in Luccio's barely legible scrawl. The message, she reported, was that he had left at seven that morning for Pittsburgh for a second interview at the university.

"You'd think he'd have let you know," I said.

"Apparently he phoned," she said.

I said, "You'd think he'd have kept phoning."

"He did," she said quietly. "I was out all night." She blew a wisp of hair off her forehead and said, "He had to catch the early bus; it was the only one today. He'll be back mid-week. He wants us to leave the suitcase."

NEAR VINELAND, we stopped in a park and ate the lunch that we were supposed to have eaten with Luccio. But in his absence, and with a whiff of deceit in the air, it wasn't much of a picnic. We walked down a wooded path that wound along the base of the Niagara Escarpment. As we crossed a small bridge, Lucy took my arm, and we stopped and, for a few seconds, held one another. "I'm sorry," she said again.

The afternoon was hot, and when we got to her apartment she ran a bathtub of water and a minute later called me in. A few minutes after that, wrapped in a black towel, she led me into the bedroom, where I took off my clothes and lay down beside her on the sheets.

I fell asleep in the twilight and awakened near midnight, alone in the bed. I wandered into the kitchen in my jeans and found her reading at the table in her bathrobe. "Oh!" she exclaimed as she looked up. "You surprised me!"

A minute later, she told me she had a confession to make. She closed her book and said, "You're not going to like me."

"Then don't tell me."

"The reason I'm telling you," she said, "is that you were very kind to do what you did today," and she explained that she'd known all along that Luccio wasn't going to be in Buffalo. I looked at her skeptically, and she said, "You hate me, don't you?" She put her book in front of her face in mock, or perhaps genuine, shame.

I said, "Why didn't you just tell me?"

"I didn't feel comfortable asking you to go all that way when he wasn't going to be there."

"I would have gone anyway."

"I know you would."

"So why didn't you?"

She stood up, and I asked if Luccio had any part in what had happened. I wondered about the contents of his letter.

"He knew I was going to ask you; it was his idea. But he didn't know I was going to tell you he'd be there."

"Are you telling me the truth?"

"I am," she said.

"So, where is he?"

"In Pennsylvania—you don't trust me now, do you?"

"I don't know."

"Well, I'm telling you what happened."

I told her I'd like to have seen Luccio.

"And he'd like to have seen you."

I said I wasn't sure about that.

"Meaning what?"

"Meaning what I said."

"That's not very nice."

I told her I thought it was true, and asked what had happened at Imperial.

"I told you what happened."

"You said it was undecided."

"It is," she said, at which point I told her I had phoned the company looking for Luccio and that they'd said he wouldn't be joining them.

"So what are you asking me for? Do you know what?" she said.

"Tell me."

"I think it's time you got going—I don't have anything else to say."

"I don't either," I said.

She stuffed her hands into the pockets of her bathrobe and, without looking at me, said, "I'm sorry, Charlie—I'll have Luccio phone you."

"If it happens, it happens."

As I turned to go, she reached out and grabbed my arm. Her voice softened and she made me promise that I'd never tell Luccio what had gone on in the apartment that afternoon.

I said, "It'd be nice to think I might get the chance."

"And you will," she said. "I'll make it happen. But you mustn't tell."

THE NEXT morning, in heavy rain, my car refused to start. I took the bus to the cemetery, arrived late and was put to work in the maintenance shop, applying gold-coloured lacquer to an elaborate concrete outer vault that was to be used the following day. The thing was big enough for a stack of bodies, and on the crest of its arched lid was the likeness of an open book, presumably the Lamb's Book of Life. On it, I was to apply neat lines of letters forming the dead person's name and the message "Love

Eternal" and a biblical reference, Psalm 46:10. All of which was
no more or less than the usual freakish provision for the arrival
of the dead at Willowlawn Everlasting.

At break, Peter informed me that the funeral was going to be
a corker—a seventeen-year-old girl had died of bone cancer. He
had been told to expect four school buses of teenagers.

I blew a reefer under the eaves of the chapel, out of the rain,
and feeling as remote as a star went back into the shop to apply a
second coat of paint. The teenager's death was made calculably
more ominous for me by her condemnation to the vulgar airless
crypt that I was in the process of decorating and in which she
was on the cusp of spending eternity. Hogjaw came in, as stoned
as I, and for a moment, on a whim, I jumped into the box and
struck a surfing pose, and jumped out.

"Lie down in it," he said, and I stepped back in and lay down.

"You look good," he said.

"I'm alive," I said. "It doesn't count."

"You're stoned is what you are."

"You get in," I said as I got out, and he stepped in and lay
down and shut his eyes.

Scotty had told me that from the age of forty the actress
Sarah Bernhardt had slept in the coffin in which she would
eventually be buried. He had read it in *Midnight*. I mentioned
it to Hogjaw, who said he thought people could do "a helluva lot
more in coffins" than they do.

I asked him "Like what?" and he said. "All they do now is rot
and go to hell." He opened his eyes and asked if I believed there
was an afterlife, to which I responded that it was a nice idea, one
that I had once held inviolable, but that I no longer knew. I asked
for his own views on the age-old stumper, and he said, "There is
as long as we're alive—after that, what the fuck does it matter?"
He closed his eyes again and held up his hands as if to receive
the blessing of the Holy Spirit. He said, "As far as I'm concerned,

this is all there is . . . this box . . . this dope . . . this gawdam fucking graveyard." He stood up, stepped out of the vault and brushed the concrete dust off his clothes. "And this dead teenager," he said, and he looked at me and rapped his knuckles on the side of the vault. "I hope I'm wrong for her sake."

"I hope you are, too," I told him.

"If I am," he said, "I'll be the first guy in hell to admit it."

I APPLIED the letters meticulously but used a little too much glue, allowing a few of them to drift out of line on the slightly bevelled surface. After break, I redid the lot of them, including the scriptural injunction, "Be still, and know that I am God." Then I rolled another joint, and walked out into the Garden of the Blessed Redeemer, where Denise was trimming stones. We smoked and sat for a few minutes, at one point touching fingers in the grass. I told her about the verse on the dead girl's vault, and she told me she thought God *was* the stillness.

"God is love," she said as I got up to go.

I returned to the shop and, with the glue nearly dry, spraypainted the inscription and went over to the shed and ate a peanut butter sandwich and a couple of overripe peaches. I rolled another joint.

The sun appeared as I ate, and I spent most of the afternoon cutting grass on the sit-down mower. From time to time I sneezed, or stifled a sneeze. About an hour from quitting time my eyes began to itch and then to water, and my nose began to run. I sneezed several times in succession, then, quite suddenly, was convulsed by a sneezing fit so forceful that I had to stop the mower, get off and lean against a tree while my body rid itself of twenty, maybe thirty, violent sneezes. Within minutes, my eyes were all but swollen shut.

I slumped into the maintenance shop a few minutes before five and was greeted by howls of laughter over my appearance.

By this time I could barely see, and my nose was runny and raw. Peter diagnosed hay fever—a menace that he said had given him fits during his first four years of cemetery work. "If you wanta get rid of it," he told me perfunctorily, "you get allergy shots. It's too late this year."

I survived the night with heavy doses of nose spray and antihistamine tablets, and had to beg off mowing the following morning. Instead, I laid out graves with Hogjaw who, in Luccio's absence and with Peter's ascent into management, had become my closest companion on the job, something I could never have foreseen earlier in the summer, when in fact he had kept me at a distance, as he tended to do with the summer help.

Throughout the morning, I suffered waves not just of hay fever but of draining pessimism as we set up to bury the dead teenager. The grave, when we finished it, contained six or eight inches of greyish water, as well as a substantial ball of newspaper that Hogjaw had used to dry the digger controls. Peter had ordered Denise to polish up the lowering device, whose gleaming stainless steel proclaimed its morbid welcome to the underworld.

From behind a grove of cedars, Hogjaw and I watched the committal, a despairing locus of grief, all of it in preposterous contrast to the crowd of high-school students in miniskirts and bell-bottomed jeans, and to the bright yellow presence of the school buses.

When we had lowered the coffin into the concrete vault and had hitched cables to the gold-painted lid, Hogjaw walked to the grave, dropped onto the edges of the vault and said, "Do you want to see her?"

"No," I said, as sure of it as I have ever been of anything. "Actually, yes," I said, "I wouldn't mind," at which point Hogjaw, the master of such exertions, spread his knees so that they touched the side walls of the grave, reached down and, having manipulated the coffin latch, lifted the lid and, holding it open, stood up, so that I had an unobstructed view. I glanced around, to make sure we weren't being watched, and for the next few seconds stared into the exquisite corpse's expressionless face, a face unmarred by the tortures of disease—in fact, except for the makeup, indistinguishable from that of any dreamy seventeen-year-old. "Bye-bye now," whispered Hogjaw, and he bent over and touched the teenager's cheek with the backs of his fingers, moving her head slightly, which spooked me, sending me back-pedalling to where I grabbed the indoor-outdoor that was covering the dirt pile, yanked it off and flung it over a nearby stone. I wrenched up a lump of clay and fired it into the grave.

We lowered the vault lid, and I hastily tidied up as Hogjaw plowed clay into the hole. It might behoove my tale to report that as a child I had an irrational fear of cancer, and by twelve or so, was praying nightly that the little lump or lesion in my armpit or groin would not do me in—at least not before I had had a chance to have sex, which I thought about day and night, ago-nized over, dreamt about, sometimes to vivifying, even alarm-ing, effect. My fantasized mate in these morbid speculations was invariably a busty brunette in black lingerie—big-nippled, perhaps twenty years my senior, and well versed in the bedroom arts. At the time, I believed I might inveigle such a woman to have sex with me if she knew I was on my way out and would require the service just once or twice . . . *which is all I want, Dear Lord, please, just this five or six times.*

As I tamped the sod into place, I experienced the same para-doxical mixture of relief and guilt that I had known as a kid after witnessing some baleful violation of the natural order. She was dead of cancer—I wasn't. Meanwhile, I wondered what night-marish forces had exploded in her skull when she had found out she had the disease—wondered what unbridgeable loneliness and despair she had endured with the awareness she was going to die.

I wondered if she had ever had sex.

nineteen

A WIDE AND SHAPELY STAGE

BECAUSE THERE was no one else to do it, I went back to mowing during the afternoon and was quickly at the mercy of my sneezing and snot. At perhaps two o'clock, under a sky the colour of old asphalt, Fred came lurching across Apostles beckoning me toward him, more excited than I'd ever seen him. Thinking he'd hurt himself or run into trouble, I jumped off the mower and ran, wheezing, perhaps fifty yards to where he grabbed my arm and hustled me through a clump of birches to where we could see the skeleton of a dying elm perhaps another twenty-five yards away. On the tree's leafless upper branches, a hundred or more frantic crows had assembled—cawing, fluttering, apparently focusing their attention on a crow that sat motionless, singled out from among them. Every so often, two or three of the flock would dart at the lone crow in a flurry of aggression then quickly retreat, and another few would take up the attack. Fred understood what was happening but couldn't communicate it, repeating time and again the words *"baid crovo"* this interspersed with a variety of gestures and facial contortions.

I said, "They're crows, Fred!"

"Yah-yah, crovo!" he responded. "Baid crovo."

We watched for several minutes until suddenly the crow under attack tumbled from the tree. The others dispersed in a loose flock, except for perhaps half a dozen that circled back, settled around the fallen crow and gave it a few last jabs before flying off, their fury spent.

We walked over and found the crow dead on the ground, blood-matted wounds on its back and neck. "Baid crovo," repeated Fred quietly, bending and turning over the carcass. He took a garden trowel from his wagon and dug a narrow foot-deep hole in the soil under a nearby lilac. With a tenderness that wrenched me, he picked up the bird, smoothed its feathers with his bare fingers and slipped it into the grave.

At break I told Peter what had happened and, when Fred came in, called him over and got him to explain to Peter in German what he'd been trying to tell me. Peter listened for a minute and turned to me with a wink. "He says that crows have laws for themselves and that when one of them breaks the laws the others hold crow court and punish him."

"Yah-yah, crow cower," nodded Fred, "cower for baid crovo."

Months later, in the Ramsay Wright Zoological Labs at the University of Toronto, I would happen on a book about the behaviour of crows and other corvids, which would corroborate what Fred had explained: that crows, the smartest of birds, with their immense hyperstriata, have a rarely observed "judicial system" through which they judge their own for "deviant behaviour" or "physical deformity." The process is considered a purge on individuals whose actions or physical differences might indicate genetic mutation that could contaminate the gene pool.

AS I punched out at quitting time, Peter appeared at his office door. "Can I speak to you for a minute?" he said, and I climbed the stairs, short of breath at the effort.

Under Peter, the little upstairs office was a different cage entirely than it had been under Scotty. For the first time in perhaps forty years it was spare, it was clean—it was free of the odour of old filth. The cobwebs had been swept out of the window frame, and the window had a new screen and was open, as it hadn't been all summer. As if in perverse caricature of a past he deplored, Peter had left Scotty's decades-old truss box on the wall, in fact had given it a place of prominence beside the door (explaining that Scotty had kept the thing on-site because it was the cemetery, the exertions of Depression-era gravedigging, that had given the poor man his hernia and, by Peter's insightful deduction, had "swollen his spleen," making him such an "unforgivable fucking asshole" over the years).

On the opposite wall, by the window, he had preserved Scotty's framed photo of the wartime Victory Gardens . . . and beside it, on a shelf, had placed what appeared to be a raccoon skull and, next to it, a "juice" tumbler, another loving commemorative of Scotty's decades of bile and booze.

Over the past couple of weeks, Peter had taken to smoking cigarillos, an affectation, I assumed, of his eminent new status in the industry. He lit one now, blew the smoke at the open window, and said, "I assume you're going back to school."

I said I wasn't sure, and he told me he had a job for me if I wanted it, but that I would have to tell him within a day or two.

"Doing what?" I asked, and he said, "The same thing you're doing now, except for more money," adding that once the ground froze and the snow came, the workload was next to nothing. "Scotty invents work—I don't," he said, and explained that from the beginning of December to the end of March, the agenda consisted mainly of "clearing snow off the burial sites, and shovelling little paths." And of course digging the holes and filling them in. "December's easy," he said with no betrayal of sarcasm. "Hardly anybody dies before Christmas."

I asked if he'd heard from Luccio, and he said that somebody had called the office about his cheque—he imagined we'd see him on payday. I told him about driving Lucy to Buffalo, in response to which he blew a cubic yard of smoke into the room and declared that the pair of them "oughta have their asses kicked."

There was a clomping on the stairs, and Hogjaw appeared at the door.

"Siddown," Peter told him, and he crossed to the window and settled against the sill.

"I wanta ask you guys something," said Peter. "I want an honest answer." He paused for a moment, looked up from his desk and said, "Did either of you open the girl's coffin this morning?"

"What the fuck kinda question's that?" whined Hogjaw.

"The kind I ask when I wanta know something," said Peter.

"What if we did?"

"If you did, you did. I just wanta know."

"Well, we did," said Hogjaw. "We opened the coffin, got her out, took her over to Bongo's for lunch, took her out dancing and bought her a new fucking dress. When we got back here, we smoked a reefer and stuck her back in the ground!"

Having rid himself of his little tirade, Hogjaw folded his arms, turned and glared out the window.

"Finished?" said Peter.

"No, I'm not," said Hogjaw, spinning back toward him. "And the reason I'm not is that we didn't do a gawdam thing that you yourself haven't done a hundred times. We took a respectful peek, closed up the box and filled in the grave. What are you suggesting, that we stole her gawdam locket or something?"

"Not at all!" objected Peter. "I just wanta tell you that if you opened the box, it's the last time you're going to do it."

"Jesus fucking Christ on a flatcar," whispered Hogjaw. He

looked at me, then at Peter. "Welcome back, Scotty! Shall I go out and get a bottle of cheap Scotch to celebrate your return?"

"Cheap wine might be more your speed," said Peter. "Meanwhile, if you'll just shut up for half a second, I'll tell you what's going on."

"What's going on?"

"You're fired," deadpanned Peter.

"I quit!" said Hogjaw, flipping up his sunglasses. "And I'm going straight to the gawdam union to tell them what's been happening around here all these years."

"Now look who's playing gawdam Scotty!"

The gist of his concern, explained Peter, was that an order had come down from headquarters—the operation, under him, was to be cleaned up and cleaned up immediately. No more messing with the graves. No more loose bones. No more transfers ("transfer" being the operative word for the emptying of an unmarked grave). "Al wants the whole gawdam Quarry filled in and capped."

"With what, more Scotch bottles?" scoffed Hogjaw, to which Peter responded that he had already ordered two hundred cubic yards of crushed limestone.

"Which should fill about a third of it," said Hogjaw.

"If it doesn't fill it," shrugged Peter, "I'll order another two hundred. And if that doesn't do it, another two hundred after that."

"And is Al going to come over and do the work?" said Hogjaw.

"No, you are," said Peter.

"The fuck I am," said Hogjaw. "Does Al know what's in there?"

"Of course," said Peter.

"Does he know what the rates are for messing with that shit?"

"No, but I do," said Peter.

"And are you gonna pay them?" brightened Hogjaw, to which Peter replied that he had every intention of making Hogjaw "a very wealthy gravedigger."

AFTER WORK, I drove straight out to Lucy's and found her packing up her kitchen. I asked what was happening, and she said a one-bedroom apartment was coming open, and that if Luccio wasn't going to be around she didn't need the second bedroom. She seemed happy enough to see me, but was more concerned about her conduct of the previous weekend than over my questions about Luccio. At length she told me he'd be home Friday, that Immigration had extended his visa. But she was unhappy about his prospects, about the fact she couldn't do more for him.

"Will you promise to have him call me?"

"Does he have your number?"

She fetched a pencil from the kitchen table, and I wrote it on a grocery receipt, and she put it on the counter without looking at it.

A few hours later, I awoke from a confused and sordid dream in which Luccio appeared in the uniform of a World War II Italian soldier. After repeated attempts to engage him in conversation, I realized, to my dismay, that he was dead, although not so dead that he couldn't wheedle me into opening a vault that he promised contained the "living body and soul" of a teenage girl. I lifted the lid with great difficulty, appalled to discover not a young woman but a wasted cadaver, a little old man of ambiguous race, whose leathery forehead bore the embossed message, "Be still, and know that I am God." When I turned to Luccio to protest, he, too, had been reduced to a corpse, the shrivelled presence of which sent me running, frightened, along a torch-lit path that meandered among open graves, each of which required a balletic leap if I was to avoid what in the dream had been presented to me as my inevitable and godless fate.

The next day, wracked by hay fever, I told Peter that I had decided not to stay, that I was going back to school.

"When?" he said matter-of-factly.

"I guess Wednesday," I told him, to which he reacted with the merest of shrugs.

WHEN I hadn't heard from Luccio by Sunday, I called the apartment and got a recorded message that the phone was out of service. On Tuesday evening, imagining that the phone company had cut the service for overdue bills, I drove over to the apartment and knocked on the door. When no one answered, I looked for the caretaker, and he told me that "the brother and sister" had moved out Saturday, owing two months' rent. He said the lock had been changed and that some of their stuff was still inside.

"What sort of stuff?" I said.

"Just some books, a few boxes."

He explained, without antipathy, that, while he didn't make the rules, if "Miss Poochy and her brother" were to pay the overdue rent, plus any rent the company might lose because they hadn't given sufficient notice, they could legally get their things at any time within six months—"After that, I burn everything," he said. "Throw it all in the incinerator."

"They had a buncha *my* books in there," I said, recalling four or five books that Luccio had borrowed over the course of the summer. "Would you let me go in and get them?"

"I've got nothing against you," he said with a shake of his head, "but if I were to let you or anybody else in there, I'd get fired."

I fished into my jeans for a five-dollar bill (a twenty-four of beer), tucked it in his shirt pocket and we were on our way upstairs.

To say the place was grubby would be to insult grubs, strewn as it was with newspapers, and dust balls and old pizza boxes.

The shower curtain had been ripped down and thrown over the toilet, and an old sheet, soiled by a single spot of brown blood, lay puddled against the bathroom door. "It's gonna take me a day just to clean the place, let alone paint it," said the caretaker, peering into the bedroom. Within a step of where a ripped and battered box spring was propped against the wall, a half-dozen dill pickles had been dumped onto the floor. The venetian blind was hanging loose at one end, and part of a can of white paint had been spilled across the bedroom floor.

"Musta been quite a party," I joked, to which my host responded, "Oh, you bet it was—the guy across the hall threatened to call the cops."

For a few seconds I stood gazing at the fastidious little caretaker in his pristine T-shirt and creased khaki pants. Eventually I said, "There was a party?"

"There sure was," he said, and he explained that he hadn't heard the noise from his basement apartment or he would have been up here "banging on the door." I followed him into the living room, and he added that by the time he came up to the apartment on Sunday morning to collect the overdue rent, "Miss Poochy and her brother" had disappeared. "This is what I found," he said. "Every light in the place was on."

I walked into the kitchen and stared out the window into the alley, wishing I had a reefer. And somebody to smoke it with. On the counter lay the grocery receipt on which I had written my phone number.

"Do you see your books?" said the janitor.

"I don't," I said, and thanked him for letting me in.

In no time, I was out of the building and racing down Avenue Road, then along the 401—as ever, it seemed, on my own, feeling peevish and indignant, hurt in ways that, at that point in my life, I did not even have the vocabulary to name.

THE FIRST loads of crushed limestone arrived shortly after eight the next morning, and, perhaps appropriately, I spent much of my last day on the job tromping around the Quarry, knee-deep in compost and green bottles—and, of course, somewhere deeper down, the remains of old rough boxes and the carcasses of those who for one reason or another had been turned out of their graves. The place had always smelled of decomp and swamp water, cut with cedar and old roses, but never more so than today, as the loads of crushed stone compressed the last musky gases out of it all. According to Peter, the morning marked the first time in his dozen years at Willowlawn that a human being had actually descended into the Quarry and mucked around in it. At one point, in a place where there were no bottles, I stepped on something angular in the organic depths, and leapt away from it, furiously shovelling limestone in behind me.

I spread stone until the dust from it had impregnated my clothing, my hair, my nostrils, my throat and lungs, leaving me powdery grey and wheezing in asthmatic fits. As Hogjaw had predicted, the first two hundred yards weren't half enough, and by break the second two hundred were on their way from a stone quarry north of the city.

Just after eleven, Peter came up to the edge to say Denise would be joining me in a few minutes, and that she would be expected to work to the standards of the men—which, with the exception perhaps of Fred's laudable habits, were the equivalent of no standards at all.

Under no circumstances, said Peter, was I to mention to Denise what I knew about the Quarry or its role in the cemetery's past.

"What are you gonna do," I laughed, "fire me?"

"No, kill you," he said.

Denise arrived, and together we compacted the past—shunting and levelling and rasping, until eventually she, too, was a dusty spectre with sweaty armpits and a growing antipathy toward Boot Hill.

At noon hour, I went to the liquor store and bought a dozen bottles of Heineken and offered them around. As usual, everyone looked to Peter for approval, and he gave it with a shrug. But he didn't take one himself. He did, however, offer me a job the next summer, with the instruction that I had only to call him in March for another exciting round among the stinking classes.

At the end of the day, we shook hands, and he thanked me—was kind enough to tell me I had done a good job. I thanked him in return, and he reminded me sarcastically that I'd been earning approximately the wages of a Mexican sardine fisherman.

"From the fourteenth century," chimed Hogjaw who, having said his goodbyes, told me ruefully that I was lucky to be on my way, that he'd "fucking well" like to be going with me . . . and, furthermore, that with a wife and three kids and a mortgage— "the full fucking catastrophe," as Peter liked to call it—he expected to be planting stiffs until he was ready to be planted himself.

Fred, who looked as ready to be planted as it is possible to look and still be mulching perennials and weeding gardens, shook my hand and called Peter and told him in German to thank me for "helping him become some more times alive again."

Between protracted goodbyes, I promised myself that somewhere down the line—Christmas appealed to my sense of bonhomie—I'd drop by the cemetery and say hello (I envisioned a jocular reunion fuelled by cognac and high-end weed); I told myself that I would take an hour some day and go visit Scotty, take him dinner, cheer him up—would visit Fred if I could stand it. And that I'd look up Norman's band—what did I care whether he was a roadie or the world's greatest guitar player? Certainly, I told myself, I would seek out Luccio's story when it appeared.

As for Denise, she stood covered in dust, back straight, her lovely fruity breasts plunging into the sunlight between us. I gave her a hug and told her to let me know about her dad. She asked if I had her phone number, and I said I had it, adding that I'd call her when we were back at school.

But for reasons I can't name I never did any of those things.

The closest I came to any sort of visit was a brief exchange with Scotty one day in Loblaws on St. Clair, where I saw him seated on a ledge at the front of the store. He had lost weight and was clearly not himself, although his eyes were unchanged, afloat in their sockets, looking out at the world as if it had somehow been lost in fog. A woman, I believe his daughter, whom I recalled vaguely from her mother's funeral, approached as I addressed him. He looked at me without a smidgen of recognition, and I said to the woman, "I worked for Scotty last summer at the cemetery."

"Gawdam good worker, too," he laughed, pushing himself upright off the ledge.

"Thanks," I said. "Are you still going in to work?"

"Only when they need me," he said, and without allowing another word, his daughter led him away, brushing past me with a joyless smile aimed at no one in particular.

HAVING SAID my goodbyes, I was immediately out of my work clothes, and within seconds was in my car, powering up the main road toward the gate.

During the weeks to come, I had a succession of dreams about Willowlawn—not exactly nightmares, but not exactly not nightmares either. In one of them Luccio appeared—gaunt, ragged, unreachable—emerging from a freshly dug grave where he had apparently drowned in a few inches of slop. But he wouldn't speak or answer even simple questions about where he had been, what he was up to or why he hadn't called. In another,

Denise approached across the Garden of the Apostles, removing a kind of tunic, revealing at the moment of truth not what I had anticipated, but a wound, perhaps lung cancer, perhaps her dad's, which had marred her beautiful torso.

In the end, the dreams invariably came back to the girl in the vault, the wizened corpse emblazoned with the word of God— to my running through the cemetery in the dark, as always, both pursuing and escaping my fate.

My understanding of death in the years that followed was little different, I suspect, than it would have been had I never dug a grave or peeked at a corpse or minded coffins in a refrigerated chapel. Or dreamed my ghoulish dreams. To claim insights even today would be untruthful. When my mother died twenty years later, followed by a pair of high-school friends, both of whom said to hell with existence, I peered into their coffins and graves as if I had never seen the likes of it all, and could never have imagined such gloomy or uncompromising ends. (In the wake of my Calvinist upbringing, it would be years before I could accept that death, like any other shadow, has no depth or interior, and is unknowable except as a stoppage of the light.)

My experience of life, on the other hand, was significantly altered—particularly as it is lived against the backdrop and awareness of the inevitable. A few months after leaving Willowlawn, on a December night, contemplating that backdrop and awareness, thinking about Luccio and the rest, I took out a scribbler and began writing notes on the summer of 1969.

By the spring of 1970, I had filled three notebooks, writing down the bones in a freewheeling scrawl perhaps legible only to myself: conversations, graveyard procedures, absurdities— exits and entrances. When I visited the cemetery many years later, it seemed smaller, less vivid, than I had remembered it. But on those nights of note taking, it was a wide and shapely stage, a lurid storyboard on which for a few months under the sun I had altered the script of my life.

On a Sunday evening in February of that year, I got a call from Denise, whose dad had died—in fact was already churched and buried, in another cemetery. She apologized for not letting me know, and told me sheepishly that she had dropped out of school.

In March, Peter called to see if I intended to come back to Willowlawn. He was curt to the point of rudeness when I told him I had decided to go to Europe for a year and would be leaving in June.

On a golden afternoon in October, outside the Bureau de Poste Montmartre, in central Paris, I opened a letter from my dad, received *poste restante,* and found enclosed a newspaper obituary for Alexander "Scotty" MacKinnon. A few months later, in the SCM Bookroom at Rochdale College, I happened on a copy of the *West Coast Review* and found a story entitled "Justice for the Damned" by Luccio Pucci, who was pitched as "a notable new writer with a literary voice forged in Canada." Almost to a phrase, it was the story he had written during the gravediggers' strike. His bio note explained that he was living in southern Italy, near his home province of Calabria, and was teaching economics and American literature at the Università degli Studi di Salerno.

The story, I am proud to report, was dedicated to me.

ON THE day I went out to Willowlawn to pick up my final cheque, the city was in the midst of a languorous return to summer. The soft maples and alders along the cemetery's north and west boundaries—"the weeds" as Scotty invariably referred to them—had come extravagantly into their fall glory and resembled a firestorm of yellow and red. As I drove through the gates,

past the Garden of the Blessed Redeemer, I glimpsed a male figure in a windbreaker angling away from me over a gentle hill
that sloped down into the Garden of Remembrance perhaps a
hundred yards away. While I did not see the man's face, I was
convinced, based on his stature, that it was Luccio, who like me
had come back to pick up his pay. I stopped the car, yelled his
name and went running out after him, dodging grave markers
like a halfback avoiding tacklers. If he was in the cemetery at all,
it seemed reasonable that he should be in Remembrance, where
I believed he had grown his marijuana. However, by the time
I got to the top of the rise, from where I could see out over the
section, there was no one in sight.

I walked along the crest of the ridge, compelled by the
thought that either Luccio was on the grounds or I had gone a
little off my nut. Maybe both. A remote, perhaps idiotic, part of
me clung to the illusion that our friendship could continue, and
would have been ecstatic to see him, to light a joint, to catch up.
A more realistic part had long since given up on him.

In Apostles, I came across Hogjaw with his shirt off, tidying
a newly plugged grave. He greeted me enthusiastically, and, in
response to my asking, said he hadn't seen Luccio or anybody
else from the summer crew. He asked if I had time for a toke
and rolled a "cemetery slim," as Luccio had called the two-toke
tidbits we had often smoked in a pinch. We blew the pathetic
little thing, and sat for a few minutes on the grass in the sunlight.
Then I walked up to the office, where I asked Helena, the receptionist, if Luccio had been in for his cheque. Without so much
as a greeting, she called over her shoulder, "Anybody know if
Poochy picked up his cheque?" to which a disembodied female
voice responded that the cheque had been mailed to him "somewhere in the States."

My own munificent cheque amounted to two hundred and
thirty-three dollars, thirty of which was "vacation pay."

"You can vacation in Oshawa," said Helena, and she blew a thin blue stream of inhaled du Maurier across the counter in front of her.

Feeling a light buzz from the reefer, I walked across the parking lot and up into the Garden of the Last Supper. The sod on the grave of the teenage girl had settled as if it had never been disturbed, and the flowers were gone except for a posy of hand-picked dahlias which was lying on the grass. As I crossed Redeemer I detoured past the grave of a long-dead Irish priest, whose headstone, a favourite of mine, bore the Auden line, "Earth, receive an honoured guest."

I walked through Remembrance, feeling as unencumbered as I had felt in a long time. Thinking that my mother might enjoy them, I yanked half a dozen yellow roses out of an arrangement on a grave by the road. Twenty yards further along, I thought better of the idea and flung them into the branches of a cedar tree, inadvertently flushing an immense black squirrel.

When I started the car, Creedence Clearwater's "Bad Moon Rising" erupted from the speakers. I did a U-turn at the corner of the Garden of the Apostles of the Living Christ, raced back up the road in second gear and, leaving the joys of the cemetery behind, powered out the gate into the flow of traffic beyond.

ACKNOWLEDGMENTS

I HAVE many friends to thank for their contributions, large and small, to this book—among them, Dan Diamond, Carol McLaughlin, Lillian Napierala, Jake MacDonald, Jackie D'Acre, Kathy Beckett, George Morrissette, Vivian Palin, Rhonda Kara Hanah, Nelson King, Gerry Waldron, Scot and Anthea Kyle, Richard Cleroux, Rob Lannon, Roz Maki, Dorothy and Pete Colby, Doug Hill, Eden Robbins, Tom Hazenburg, Elizabeth Kouhi, Mary Frost, Margie Betiol, Doug Flegel, Jari and Maija Sarkka, Kevin Parkinson, Bob Kyte, John Warner and Doug Livingston.

I am particularly indebted to my friend Philip Syme, who for the past year has been a patient and generous confidant as I worked out the details of my story.

The book would not exist, of course, without my friends at Penguin Canada, all of whom deserve special gratitude—among them, the book's publicist Stephen Myers, its ever-astute production editor Sandra Tooze and my long-time friend, editorial director Diane Turbide. I also owe owe a sincere debt of gratitude to my talented and painstaking copy editor, Eleanor Gasparik, who did so much for the manuscript and to my editor, Helen Reeves, whose upbeat direction and down-to-earth literary acumen—and whose evolving friendship—have been an indispensable part of the makings of the book.

Major thanks are also due my agent, Jackie Kaiser, at Westwood Creative Artists, who for years has been my trusted adviser and friend, and whose faith in my capabilities is at the foundation of my work as a writer.

Quite apart from the specifics of this book, I would be remiss if I did not thank my sisters, Ann and Susan, and their families, for both recent and lifelong contributions to my professional and personal well-being.

Finally, I wish to thank my friend, Trish Wilson, who in a variety of ways has been as much a catalyst as anyone to the creation of the work at hand. And as always, my children, Matt, Georgia and Eden, whose love, encouragement and forbearance I could not do without.

I deeply appreciate you all.

CHARLES WILKINS is a best-selling and award-winning author with three National Magazine Awards and two American Magazine Association awards to his credit. His acclaimed non-fiction includes *The Circus at the Edge of the Earth*, *Walk to New York* and *A Wilderness Called Home*, all of which were *Globe and Mail* Top 100 books. He is also the co-author, with Don Starkell, of the international bestseller *Paddle to the Amazon*. Wilkins divides his time between Thunder Bay and Muskoka, Ontario. Follow his latest adventure at http://bibluerow.com/.